Name___________

*The Ward Method*

*Music Instruction for Catholic Schools*

*by Justine Ward*

STUDENT WORKBOOK III

for use with

# THINK & SING

Revised Edition 1982

Containing written exercises in:

Intonation

Rhythm

Notation

Creative Activity

Sight Singing Drills

Prepared by Theodore Marier



Distributed by

Catholic University of America Press
Washington, D.C.

# Lesson 1 Intonation

Review Mode of LA, Plagal Range (Natural Minor)

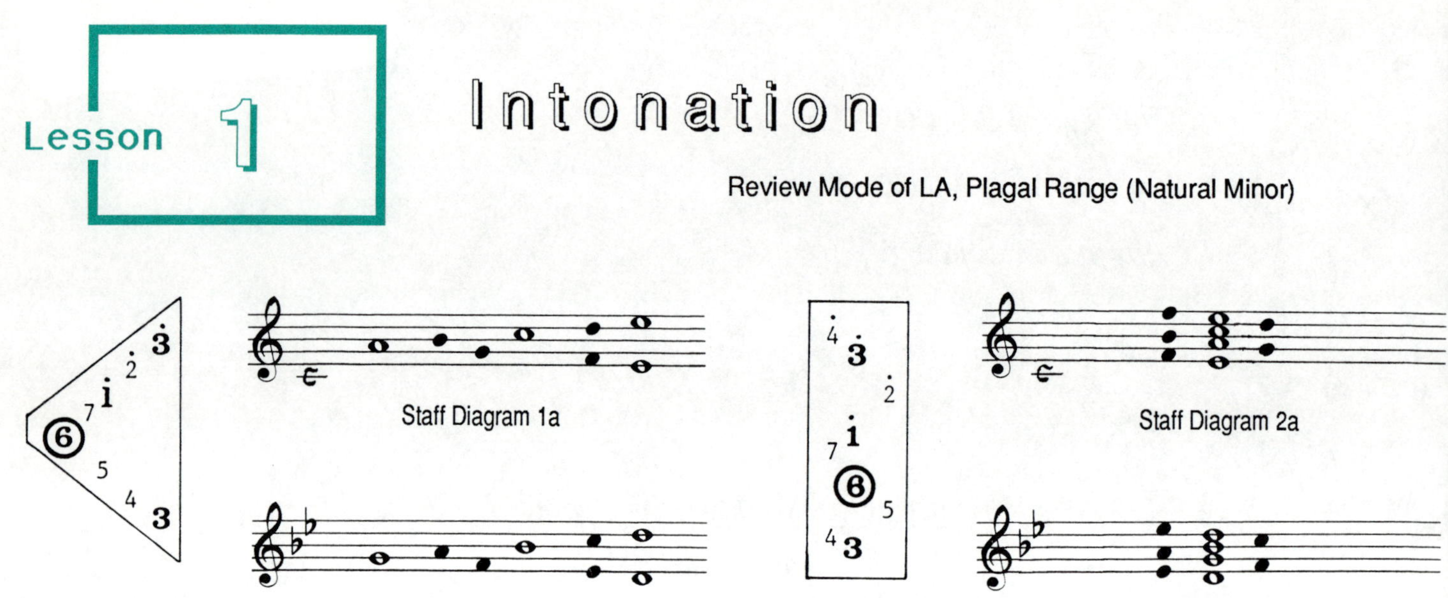


**Ear and Eye Tests**

# Rhythm

Rhythm Patterns - **Series 1, Schema I**: Beginning on Up-Pulse

Study each rhythm pattern as follows:

1) **Metrical Gesture I** and **Metrical Language**.
2) **Rhythm Gesture II** or **IV** (Binary) and **Metrical Language**.
3) **Rhythm Gesture II** or **IV** (Binary) and Melodic Application

**Dictations**

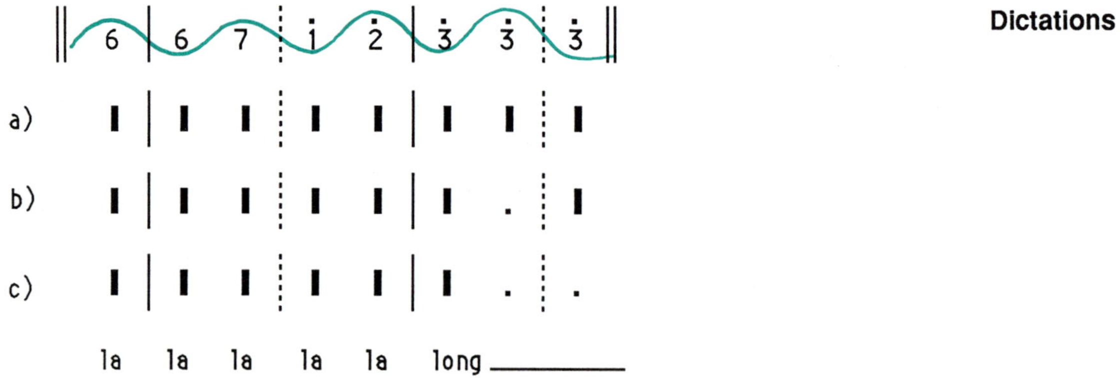


*See* Melody No. 1 *and* **THE COMING OF NIGHT** *in* Book III Songbook

Rhythm Patterns - **Series 2 Schema II**: Beginning on Down-Pulse Rhythm Gesture IV (Binary)

**Dictations**

*see* Melody No.2 *and* **LORD, WITH GLOWING HEART** *in* Book III Songbook

Rhythm Patterns - **Series 3 Schema III**: Beginning on third pulse of a four-pulse measure

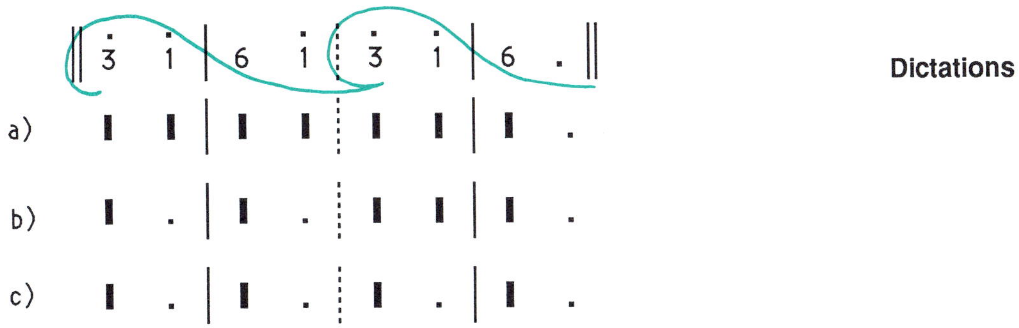

**Dictations**

*see* Melody No. 3 *and* **MORNING** *in* Book III Songbook

> If a melody begins with a full measure, it will end with a full measure. If a melody begins with an incomplete measure, the remainder of the opening measure will be found at the end.

# Notation

**Transcriptions**

## 1. PITCH

1. Transcribe Mode of LA - Plagal Range to Staff Notation.

Numbers to Notes

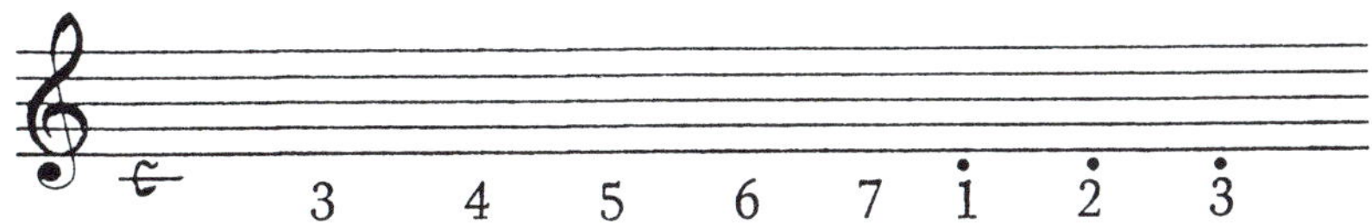

2. Transcribe Mode of LA - Plagal Range to Number Notation.

Notes to Numbers

*Continued*

## 2. RHYTHM

Pulse Lines to Notes

Numbers to Notes

## 3. MELODY

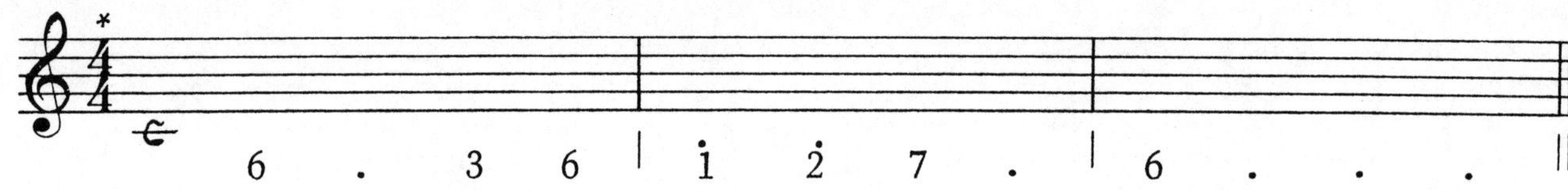

6 . 3 6 | 1 2 7 . | 6 . . . ||

*The two numerals placed one above the other at the beginning of a melody are called the Time Signature. The upper numeral tells us that there are four pulses in each measure; the lower numeral tells us that the quarter note ♩ or its equivalent, is the unit of pulsation.*

# Creative Activity

Melodic Applications

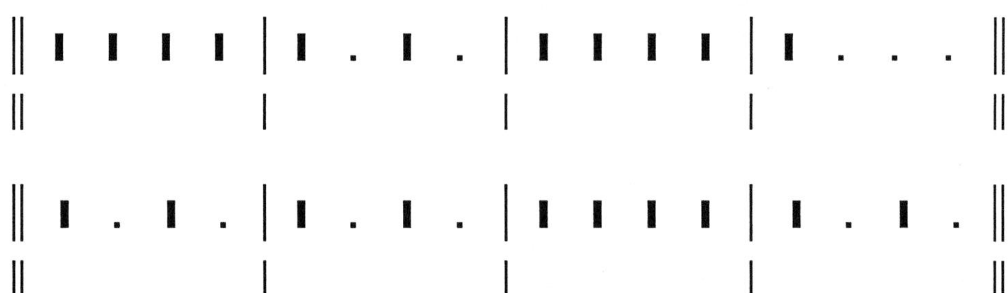

Composing a Melody for a Text First mark accents on the stressed syllables. Add measure bars before each accent. Add melody in Mode of LA. End on LA.

How should I a plan- et know From an- y oth- er star?

By its con- stant stead- y glow In the skies a- | far.

*N. H. Dole*

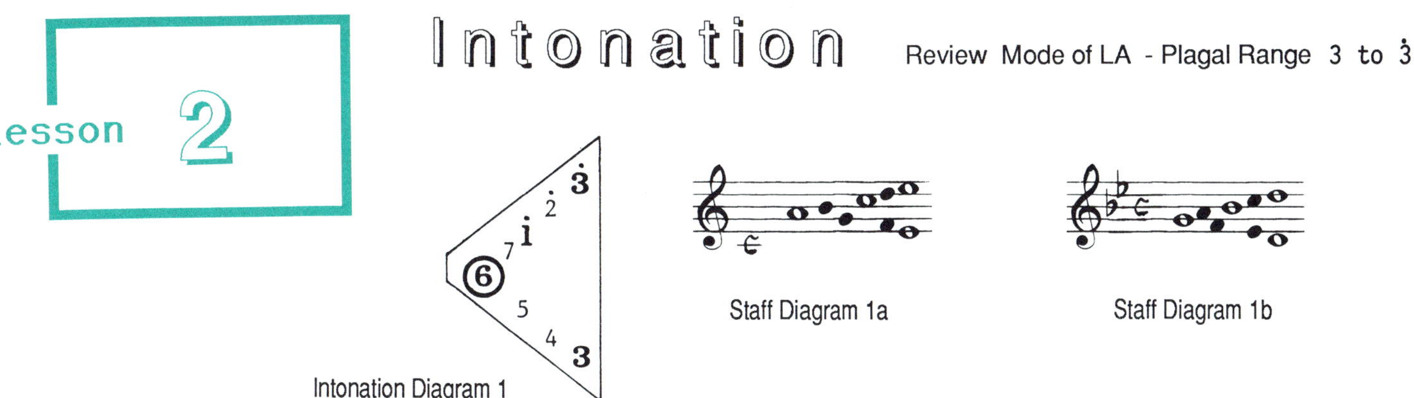


# Lesson 2

## Intonation

Review Mode of LA - Plagal Range 3 to 3̇

Intonation Diagram 1

Staff Diagram 1a

Staff Diagram 1b

**Ear and Eye Tests**

## Rhythm

4/4 Time - **Schema I** Beginning on Up-Pulse
Eighth Notes (Half-Pulse Notes)

Rhythm Patterns **Series 4**

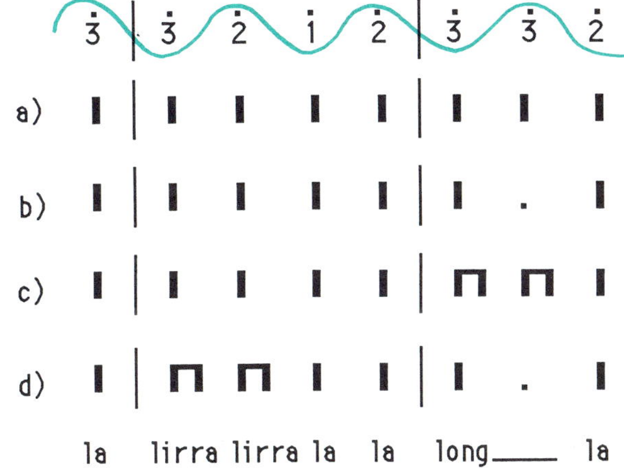


Practice Rhythm Patterns as in Book One:

1. Read each pattern using **Metrical Gesture I** and **Metrical Language**;
2. Name notes using **Metrical Gesture I**;
3. Sing notes using **Metrical Gesture I**;
4. Sing notes using **Rhythm Gesture I** or **II**.

*Space for Rhythmic Dictations on Page 7.*

*for improvisation*

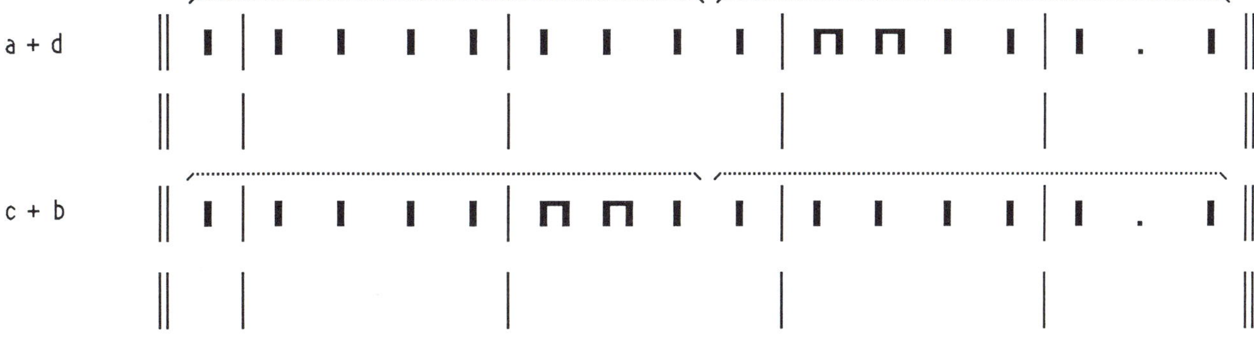

# Notation

## Transcriptions

*Review* Four positions of the DO Clef for Major and Minor Keys
Tempo Indications (Italian) Allegro, Moderato, Andante
Transcriptions

1. Transcribe each of the following from Number Notation to Staff Notation. Sing each fragment several times.

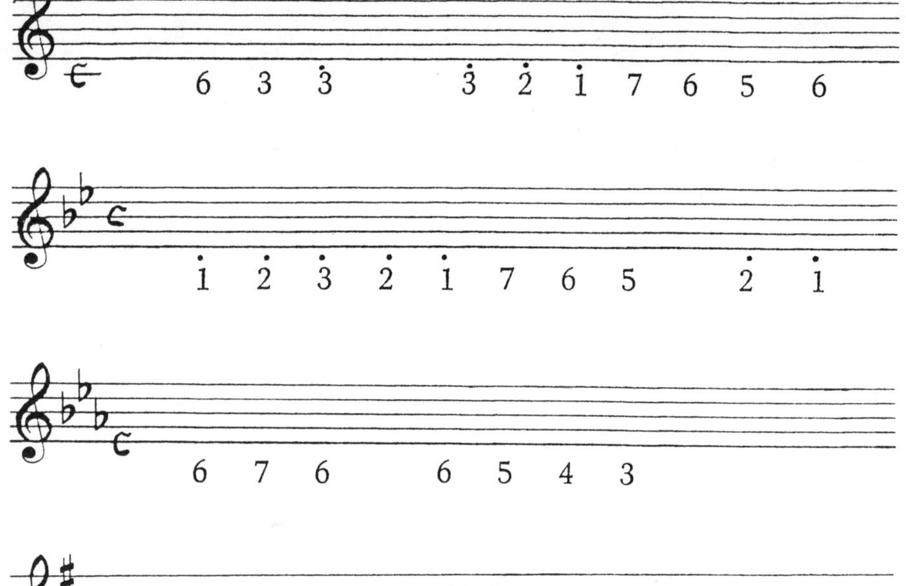


Preparation for
**HARVEST SONG**
Minor key

Preparation for
Melody No. 4
**SEPTEMBER**
Major Key

2. Conventional tempo indications:

Allegro - Joyfully, quickly, brightly
Moderato - Moderately, movement at a comfortable pace
Andante - Slowly but with a quiet forward movement

Notice tempo indications given for songs in this lesson.

3. Practice in changing clefs. Sing the following line "Andante" using note names.

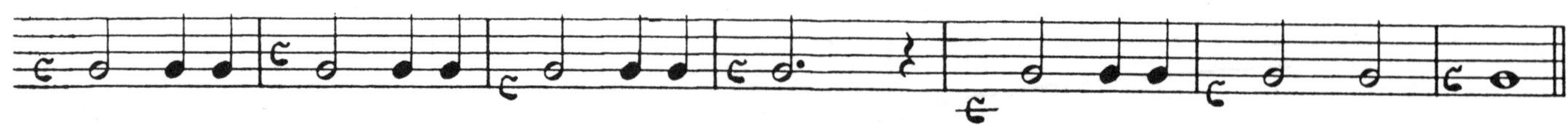

# Creative Activity

Composing Statement-Response in Minor Mode
Composing a Melody for a Given Text

Written Compositions

1. Compose an appropriate response to each of the following statements

2. Compose a melody in the Minor Mode for the following text:

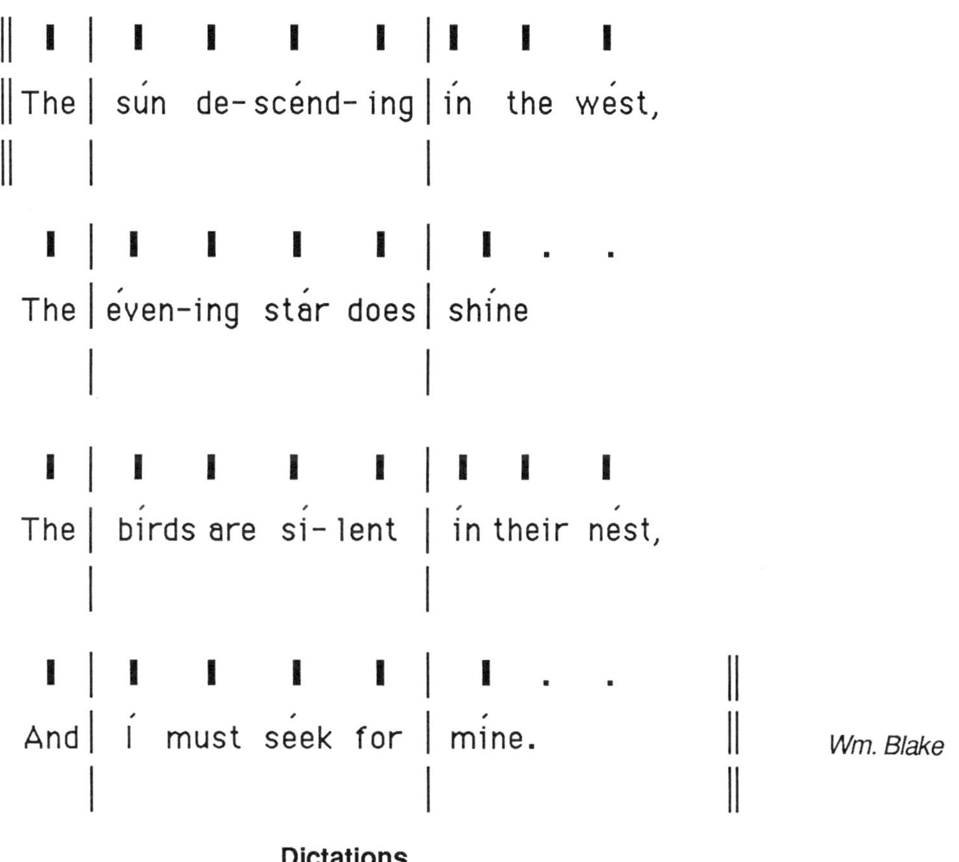


**Dictations**

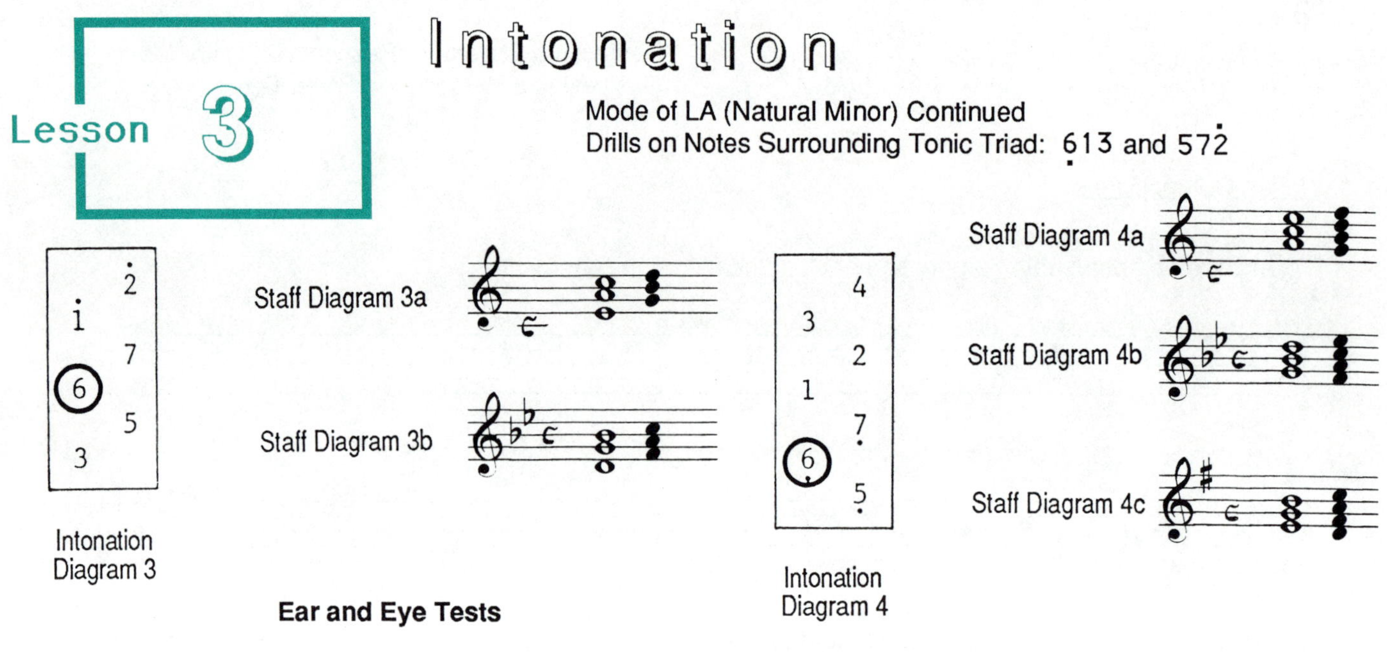


# Rhythm

4/4 Time - **Schema II** Beginning on Down-Pulse
Eighth Notes (Half-Pulse Notes)

Rhythm Patterns **Series 5**

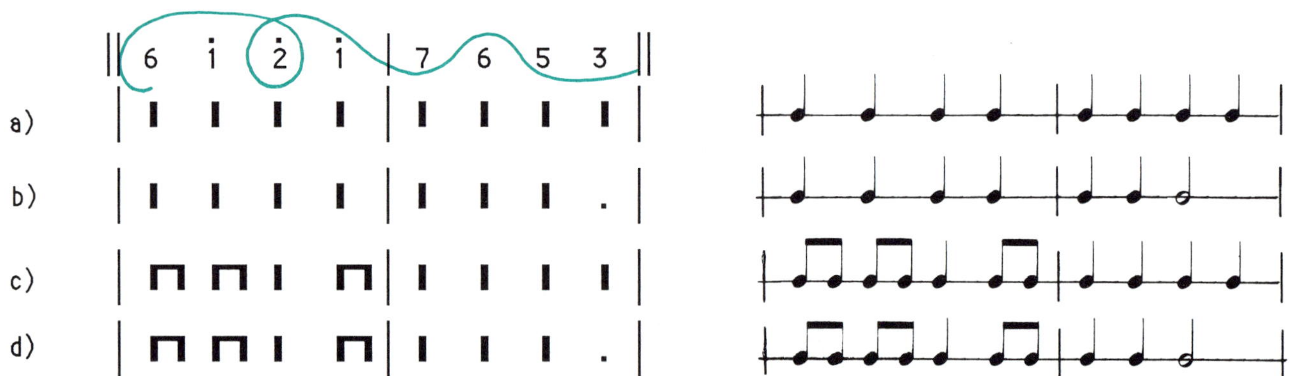


1. Read Rhythm Patterns using **Metrical Gesture** and **Metrical Language**
2. Sing Rhythm Patterns using notes given with **Arsis-Thesis** (Rhythm Gesture IV)
3. Improvise melodies to the rhythms

## Rhythmic Dictations

# Notation

Four Positions of DO Clef continued

### Transcriptions

1. Find the place of DO and transcribe to Number Notation:

2. Find the place of DO and transcribe to Staff Notation:

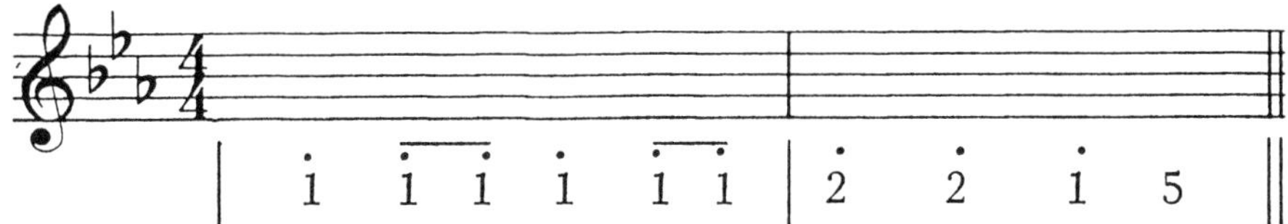


3. Find the place of DO and transcribe to Number Notation:

4. Find the place of DO and transcribe to Staff Notation:

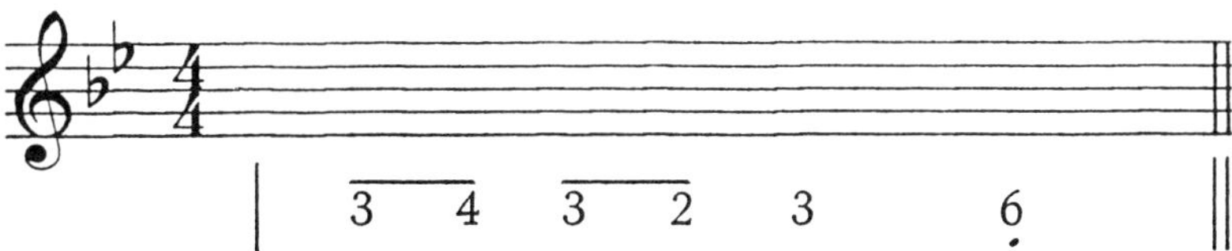

# Creative Activity

Composing Answering Statements to Phrases
Taken from Songs of the Chapter
Conversations in Minor Mode

1. Compose a suitable response to the following statement taken from the Spanish Carol (Melody No. 9). End on the Final LA (Minor Mode)

2. Compose a suitable response to the following statement taken from the Finnish Folk Song **HARK TO THE CUCKOO**. (Major Mode)

3. Two students engage in a musical conversation in the Minor Mode. Improvisation must be made to the rhythm pattern given below or to one of the other rhythm patterns of this chapter. The conversation is over when the last note of a response is the Final of the mode: LA

# Intonation

Presenting SOL Sharp: SE
Preparing for the Harmonic Minor Mode

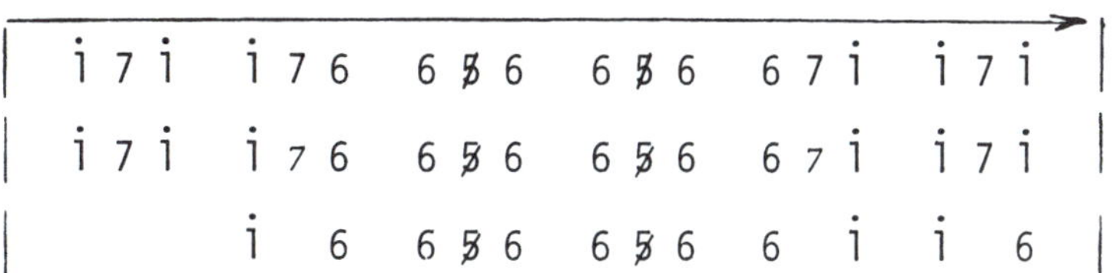


*Approaching SE downward from DO*

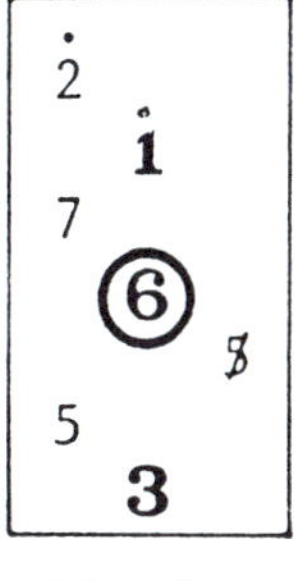


Intonation Diagram 5

Staff Diagram 5a

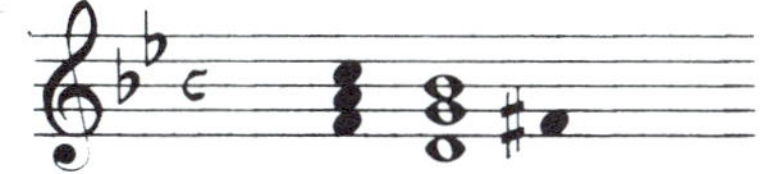

Staff Diagram 5b

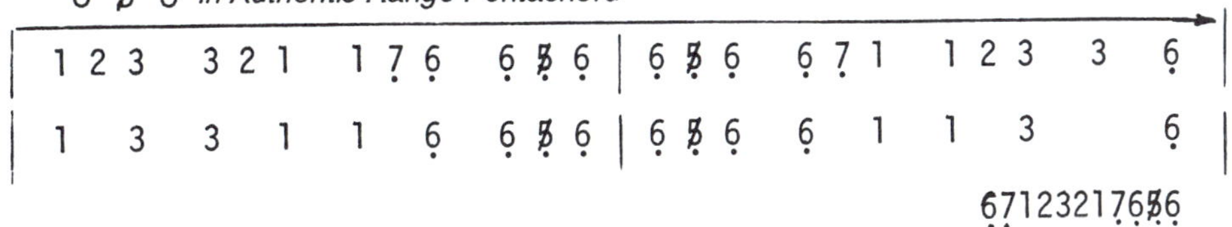


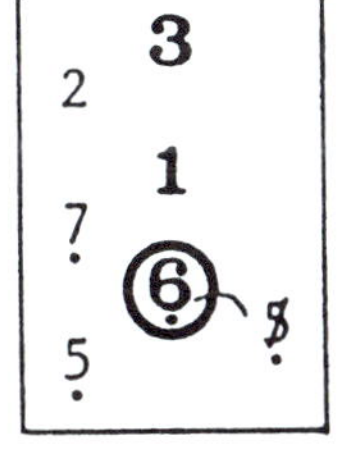


Intonation Diagram 6

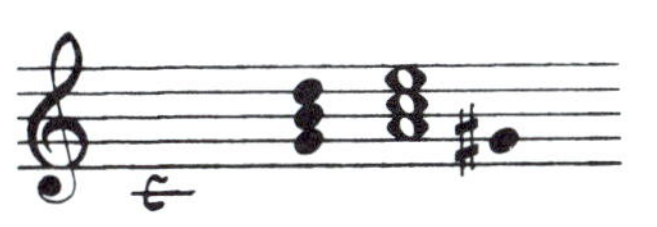

Staff Diagram 6a

Staff Diagram 6b

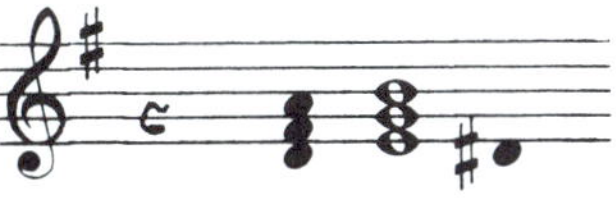

Staff Diagram 6c

Preparing for Staff Notation Melodies in the Harmonic Minor Mode
Repeat each segment several times

**Ear and Eye Tests**

# Rhythm

4/4 Time - **Schema III** with Eighth (Half-Pulse) Notes

Rhythm Patterns - **Series 6**

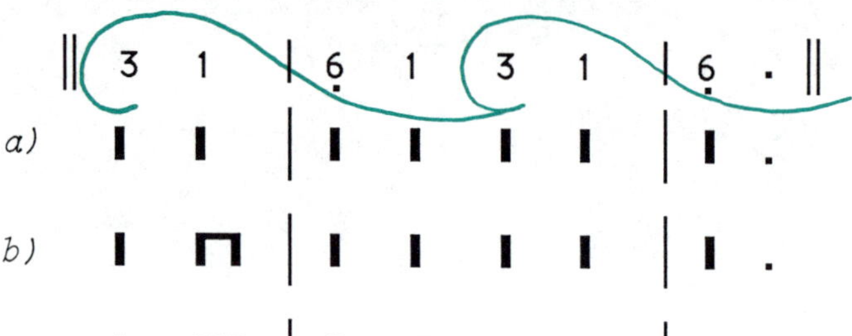


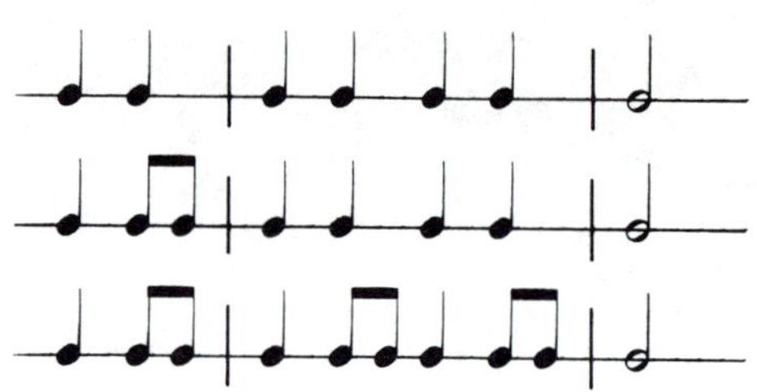

1. Read, sing and improvise according to the procedure suggested in Lesson Three

2. Improvise a melody in the Minor Mode for the following combinations of rhythms

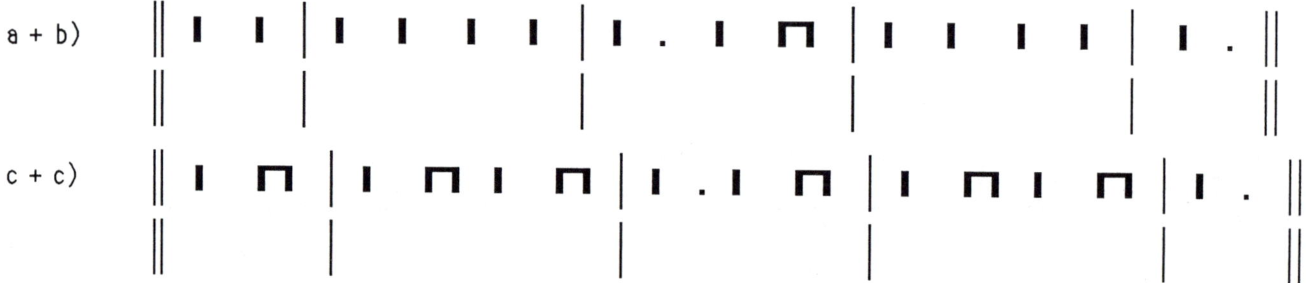


**Rhythmic Dictations**

# Notation

Function of Sharp ( ♯ ) and Cancel ( ♮ ) Signs
Transcriptions involving SE in Minor Mode
Practice in Staff Notation Reading with Changing Clefs

**MELODY NO. 12** (Excerpt)

Transcribe to Number Notation

**MELODY NO. 14**

Transcribe to Staff Notation

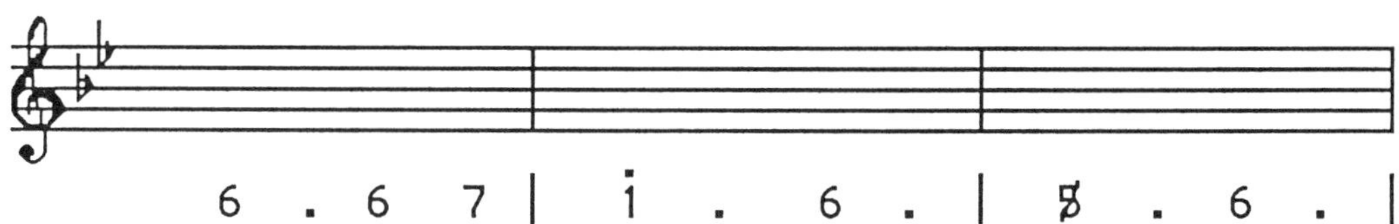


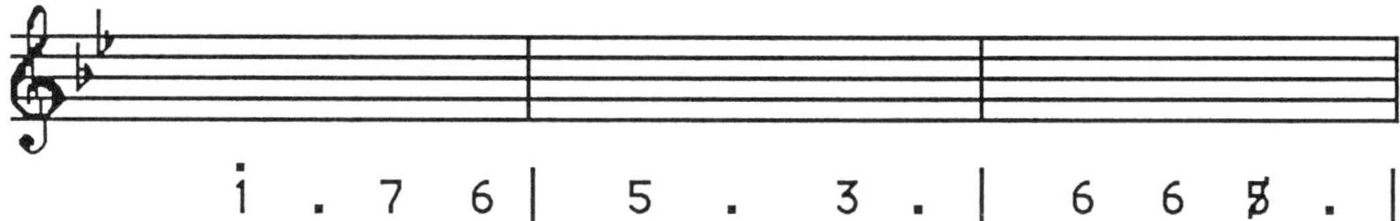


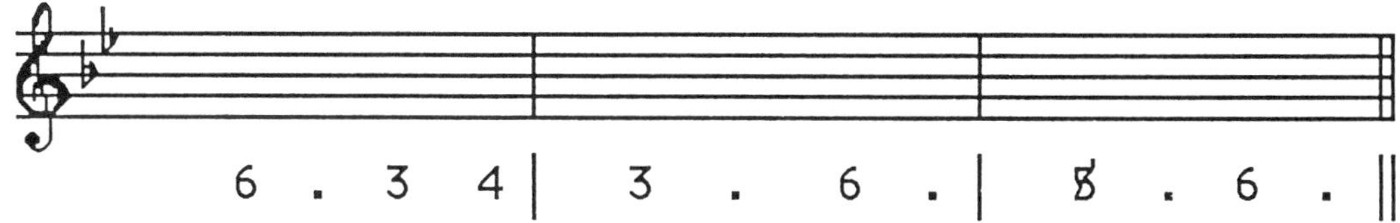


Staff Notation Reading with Changing Clefs

# Creative Activity

Composing Themes in 4/4 Time - **Schema III**
Composing a Melody for a Text

1. Compose suitable responses to each statement given

# Intonation

Drills on the Interval 6 5̸ 6 in the Minor Mode
Plagal Range

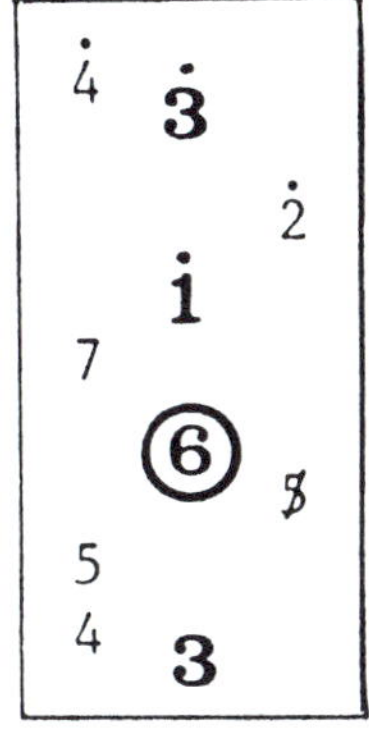


Intonation Diagram 7

Staff Diagram 7a

Staff Diagram 7b

with Intonation Diagram 7 and Staff Diagrams 7a, 7b

| | |
|---|---|
| 1̇ 7 6 · 6 5̸ 6 · 6 5 4 3 · 3 4 3 | 3 4 3 · 3 4 5 6 · 6 5̸ 6 · 6 7 1̇ · 1̇ 6 |
| 1̇ 6 · 6 5̸ 6 · 6 3 · 3 4 3 | 3 4 3 · 3 6 · 6 5̸ 6 · 6 1̇ · 1̇ 6 |

Three Compass Exercises with 5̸

| | | |
|---|---|---|
| 6 7 6 · 1̇ 2̇ 1̇ · 3̇ 4̇ 3̇ | 3̇ 4̇ 3̇ · 1̇ 2̇ 1̇ · 6 7 6 | 6 5̸ 6 · 3 4 3 · 6 5̸ 6 |
| 6 · 1̇ · 3̇ | 3̇ · 1̇ · 6 | 6 · 3 · 6 |
| 7 6 · 2̇ 1̇ · 4̇ 3̇ | 4̇ 3̇ · 2̇ 1̇ · 7 6 | 5̸ 6 · 4 3 · 5̸ 6 |

**Ear and Eye Tests**

# Rhythm

4/4 Time - **Schema I** with Eighth Notes ♫ and Dotted Rhythms ♩. ♪

Rhythm Patterns - **Series 7** Study with **Metrical Language** and **Metrical Gesture I**
Improvise melodies to each pattern

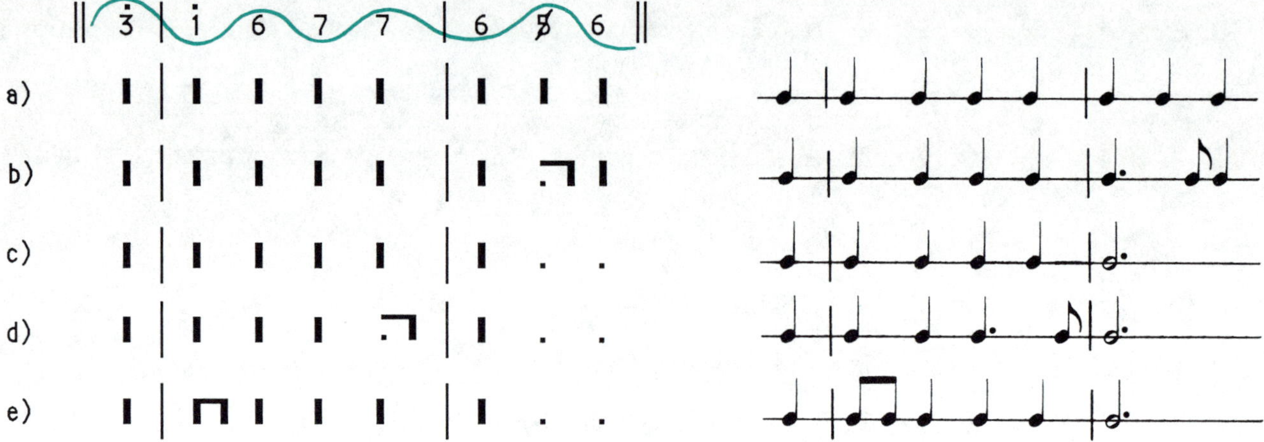


Compose melodies for the following combined patterns

**Dictations**

# Notation

DO Clef on Middle Line in Sharp Key of B (i = B)
Four Positions of the DO Clef Continued

Find correct place on the staff for each note given

Review of Four Positions of the DO Clef in LA Mode
Transcribe each 656 6$\not{5}$6 to staff as indicated

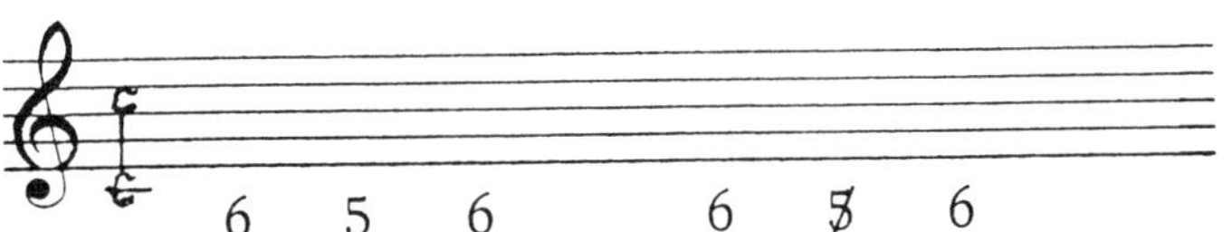


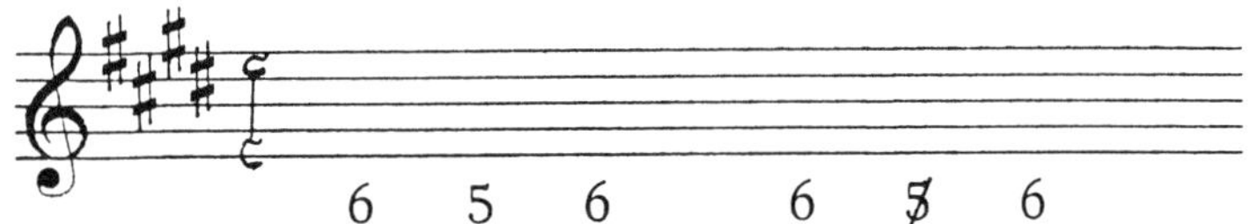


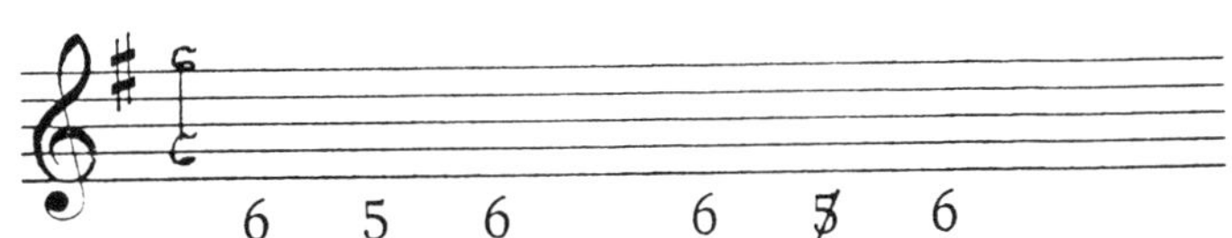


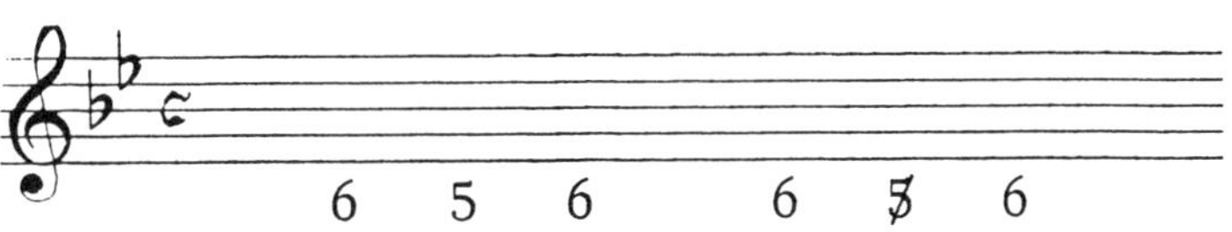


# Creative Activity

Composition and Study of Song Form [1]
"Lied" Form - A B A and A A B A

1. A B A Form

Compose a melody in A B A Form with the A Statement given (From music by F. J. Haydn)

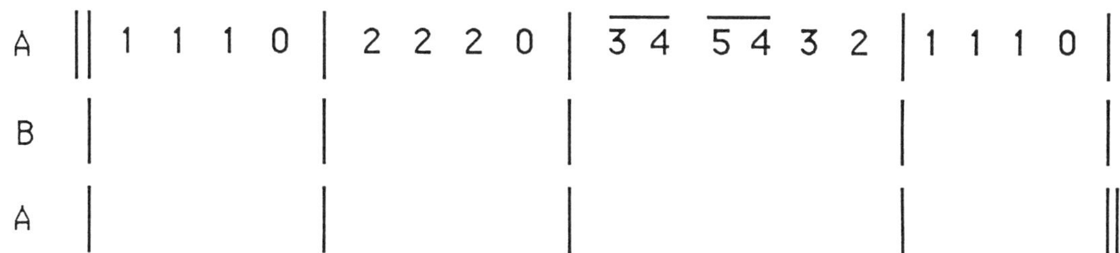


2. A A B A Form

Compose a melody in A A B A Form with the A Statement given
(Excerpt from music by Franz Schubert)

**Fine* (Pronounced "Fee-neh") means end.
***D.C.* Abbreviation of "da capo" means return to beginning.

Minor Mode - Plagal Range (Continued)
Approach to ♯5 by leap from above: 7 - ♯5
and from below: 3 - ♯5

# Intonation

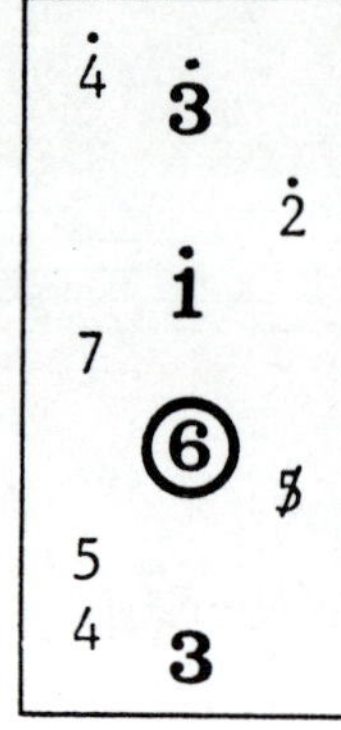


Intonation Diagram 7

| 6 7 1 2 3 1 2 7 1 6 ♯5 6 7 6 6 5 4 3 6 ♯5 6 |
| 6 1 3 1 2 7 1 6 ♯5 7 6 6 3 6 ♯5 6 |
| 6 1 3 1 2 7 1 6 7 ♯5 6 6 3 4 3 6 ♯5 6 |

**Ear and Eye Tests**

# Rhythm

4/4 Time - **Schema II** with Dotted Rhythms ♩. ♪
Conducting in 4/4 Time

Rhythm Patterns - **Series 8**

Study each of the patterns by:

- Reading with **Metrical Language** and **Metrical Gesture I**
- Making Melodic Applications
- Combining patterns
- Analyzing similar patterns in songs of this chapter
- Transcribing patterns to **Staff Notation**
- Dictations

|| 1 1 3 2 | 1 7 6 . ||

a) | I I I I | I I I . |

b) | I I I ⊓ | I I I . |

c) | I I ⊓ I | I . . . |

d) | I .⌐ I I | I . . . |

Last rhythm is a Whole Note

Dictations on Page 21

**Metrical Gesture IV** - Conducting in 4/4 Time

In order to accommodate the four pulses of the measure, the gesture contains four separate movements as shown below. The down-pulse is always the first beat of the measure.

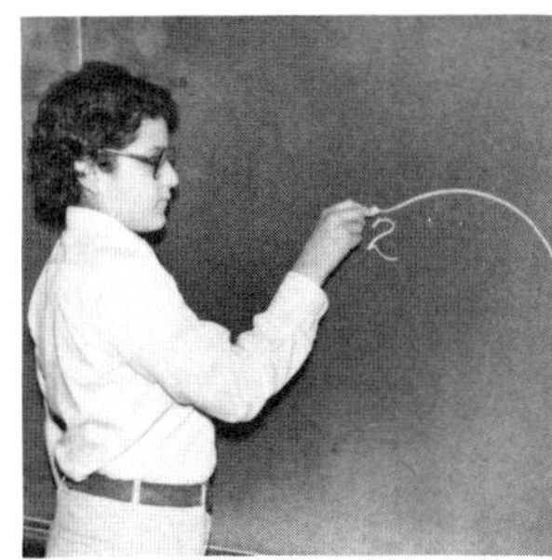

<u>DRILL</u> Conduct each of the patterns given above in Series 8

# Notation

The Cancel ( ♮ ) as a Means of Raising a Note Flatted in the Key Signature

The Measure Bar Cancels Effect of Accidentals ♮ ♯ ♭

**Transcriptions**

# Creative Activity

Composition and Study of Song Form [2]
Forms: ABAC AABB ABAb

1. The ABAC Form

2. The AABB Form

Let us consider the Melody No. 19 (Russian Folk Dance)

A = Theme A = Theme repeated B = New melody B = New melody repeated

Now compose the B theme for the following A theme:

Minor Mode

AA ‖: 1 . 6 | 1 . 2 | 3 . 4 | 3 . . :‖

BB ‖: | | | :‖

3. The ABAb Form

Let us consider Melody No. 2 (Chapter One)

A = Theme B = New Melody A = Theme b = Same melody as B but slightly changed

Now compose melodies for the missing lines below. The form is ABAb.

**Rhythmic Dictations**

Minor Mode of LA with SOL# 5̸ (SE)
Authentic Range Compass Exercises

# Intonation

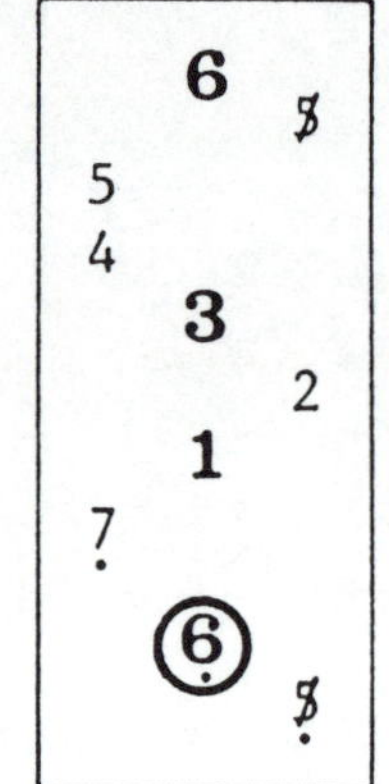


Intonation Diagram 8

Staff Diagram 8a

Staff Diagram 8b

Intonation Exercise 15 Compass Exercises Authentic Range

| | | |
|---|---|---|
| I | 6 7 6 1 2 1 3 4 3 6 5̸ 6 | 6 5̸ 6 3 4 3 1 2 1 6 7 6 6 5̸ 6 |
| II | 6 1 3 6 | 6 3 1 6 6 |
| III | [6] 7 6 [1] 2 1 [3] 4 3 [6] 5̸ 6 | [6] 5̸ 6 [3] 4 3 [1] 2 1 [6] 7 6 [6] 5̸ 6 |

**Ear and Eye Tests**

# Rhythm

Schema III 4/4 Time
Dotted Quarter and Half-Pulse Notes (Eighths)

Rhythm Patterns - **Series 9**

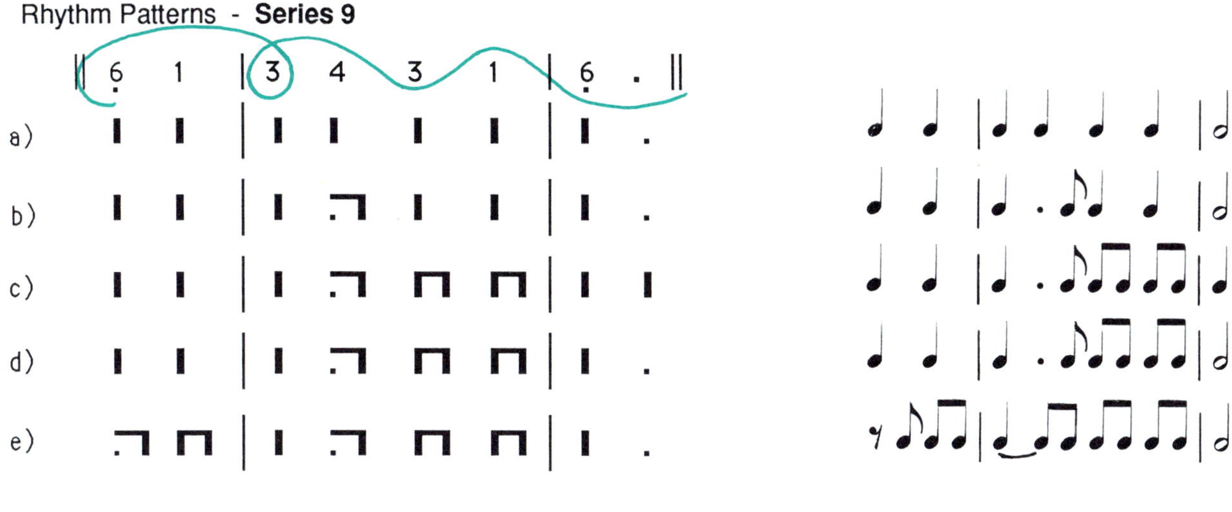


*Derived from* **A LITTLE ROBIN CAME**

**Dictations**

# Notation

Transcriptions in Mode of LA with SOL#
Sight-Singing Drills

Transcribe to Staff Notation

# Creative Activity

Assimilation of Four-line Song Forms
Improvising Complementary Phrases in LA Mode
Composing a Melody for a Given Text in DO Mode

1. <u>Assimilation of Four-Line Song Forms and Variants</u>

Example of AaBA see **FIREFLIES** in Songbook

Example of ABAC

| | | |
|---|---|---|
| ‖ 3 3 2 3 | 1 . $\underset{\cdot}{6}$ . | A |
| \| 2 2 1 2 | 3 . . 0 | B |
| \| 3 3 2 3 | 1 . $\underset{\cdot}{6}$ . | A |
| \| 3 2 1 $\underset{\cdot}{7}$ | $\underset{\cdot}{6}$ . . . ‖ | C |

see also **ONCE IN ROYAL DAVID'S CITY** and **PAT-A-PAN** in Songbook

2. <u>Improvise Complementary Phrases at B and C - LA Mode with Rhythm Schema III</u>

3. <u>Compose a Melody for a Given Text</u> - Mode of DO 4/4 Measures with Rhythm Schema III

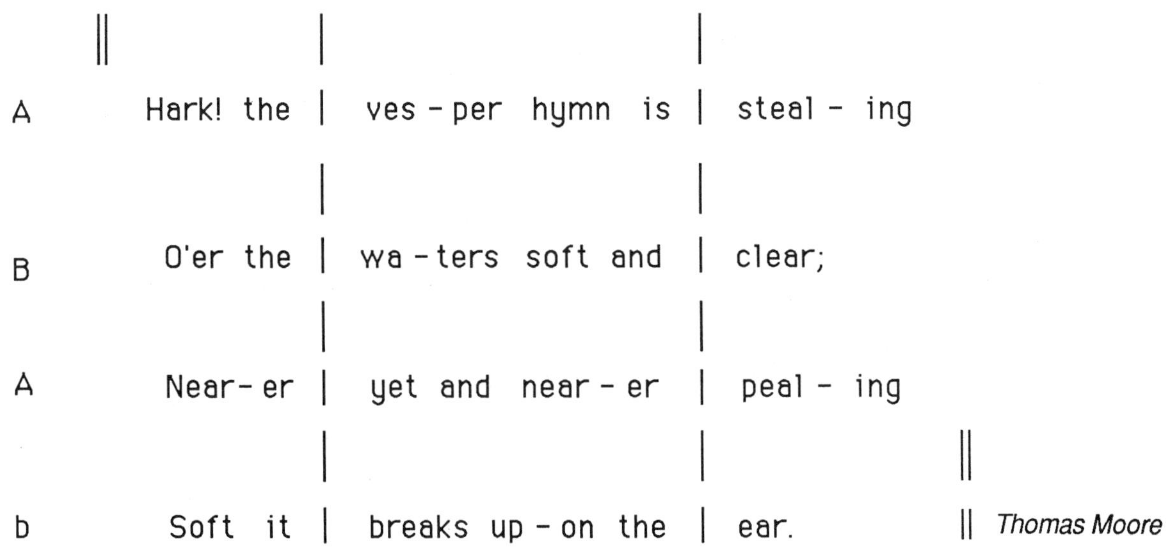

# Intonation

Comparison and Contrast of DO and LA Modes
in Authentic and Plagal Ranges

Authentic Range

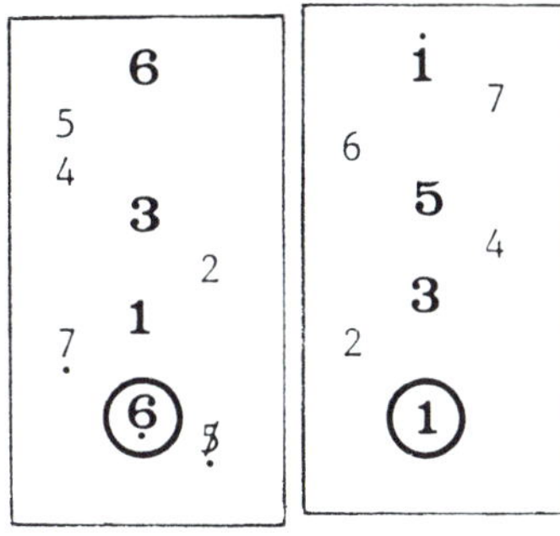


Intonation
Diagram 9

Plagal Range

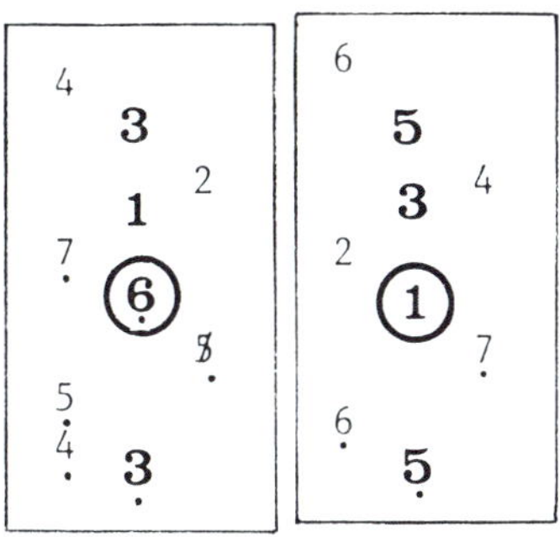


Intonation
Diagram 10

**Ear and Eye Tests**

# Rhythm

Review: Rhythm Gestures II, III
Metrical Gestures II, IV
Triplet with Eighth Notes

Rhythm Gesture II - **NOW THAT THE DAYLIGHT**

Rhythm Gesture III - **THE FIRST NOWELL**

Metrical Gesture II - **LITTLE PARTRIDGE**

Metrical Gesture IV - **CHRIST IN BETHLEHEM IS BORN**

**Dictations**

# Notation

Transcriptions in Modes of LA and DO

1. Transcribe to Staff Notation

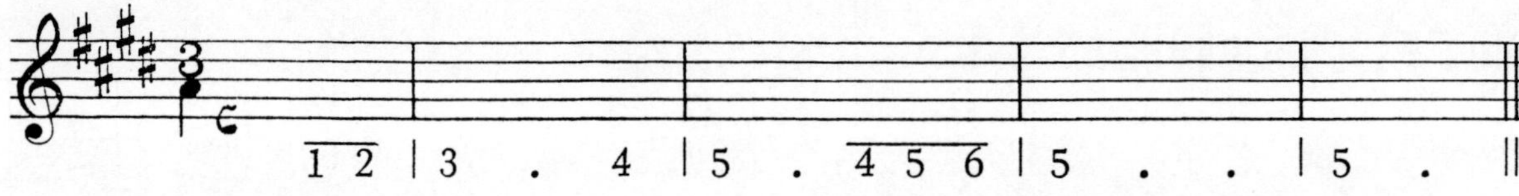


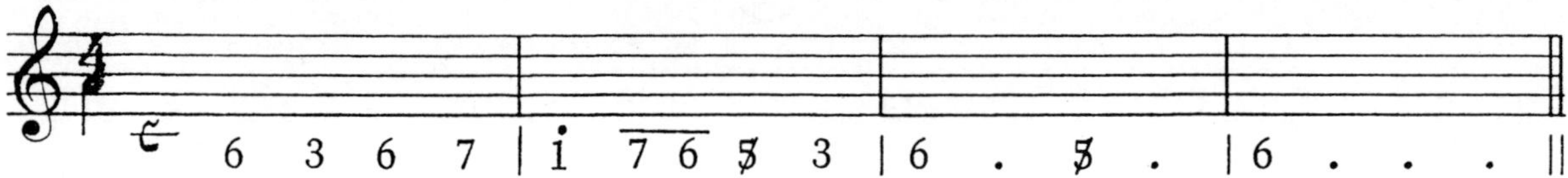


2. Transcribe to Number Notation

# Creative Activity

Study of ABCA Form in Modes of DO and LA

Notice ABCA Form of **NOW THAT THE DAYLIGHT FILLS THE SKY**

In this song the contrasting phrases are melodic. Contrasting phrases may also be rhythmic or melodic-rhythmic.

N.B. The A theme in this form must end on the Final, or Tonic, of the mode

Study and sing the two examples given below:

Exercises in Composition

1. Improvise contrasting phrases, that is, melodic or melodic-rhythmic, to each of the lines of Intonation Exercise 16 below.

a) | 1 5̣ 1 2 | 3 . 2 . | | ||

b) | 3 2 1 2 | 3 3 6̣ . | | ||

c) | 6̣ 3 6 6 | 5̸ 6 3 . | | ||

d) | 1 5 6 5 | 3 4 5 . | | ||

e) 3 2 | 1 5 1̇ 7 6 | 5 . . | | ||

f) 6̣ 7̣ | 1 3 3 6 | 3 . . | | ||

g) 5 6 | 5 1̇ 5 4 3 | 2 . . | | ||

h) 1 | 6̣ 5̣ 6̣ 1 2 | 3 . . | | ||

2. Compose missing phrases for the song below in ABCA Form.

Introducing TI Flat 7̸ - TE (TAY) in DO Mode
The Cancel Sign ♮
Exercises in Half-Step 6 7̸ 6

# Intonation

1. TI Flat - Tay - the lowered seventh degree of the DO Mode

In Number Notation, the down-stroke through the figure 7̸, indicates the lowering of that pitch by a half step 6 7̸ 6
LA TE LA

In Staff Notation, the sign for flat is ♭ It is placed to the left of a note that is to be lowered by a half-step

2. The Cancel ♮

If a key signature includes sharps, that is ♯ the lowered seventh tone of the scale will be shown as a Cancel ♮

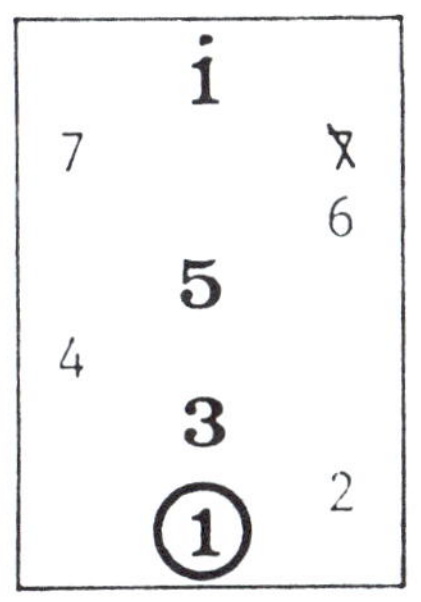


Intonation Diagram 13

Intonation Exercise 17

**Ear and Eye Tests**

# Rhythm

Review Rhythm Gesture IV (A and T) to prepare for Chant Melodies:

**WE ADORE THEE**
***BENEDICAMUS DOMINO***
**THE PENITENTIAL RITE**

Review Metrical Gesture III to prepare for:

**A VIRGIN MOST PURE**
**THE OLD WOMAN TOSSED UP IN A BLANKET**

# Notation

The Flat Sign ♭
Effect of Measure Bar
The Cancel Sign ♮
DO Clef on Line 4 of Staff
Sight Singing Drills

The Flat lowers the note beside which it stands by a half step. Its effect is automatically cancelled by a new bar-line or by the Cancel

* The Flat of the previous measure has been cancelled automatically by the measure bar
** The Flat before the second note of the measure has been cancelled by the sign ♮

DO Clef on Line 4 of the Staff

When there are two sharps in the key signature, the DO Clef is on the fourth line of the staff

Sing up and down the scale several times

Repeat each segment several times

# Creative Activity

Study of Forms Continued
AABC
Ternary Rhythm

1. Theme suggested for AABC Form *(Johannes Brahms)*

2. Compose a melody in LA Mode for the text given. Use AABC Form. End on LA.

| | | | | | |
|---|---|---|---|---|---|
| A | ‖ A | while be- | fore the | gray of | dawn, |
| A | All | on a | sum - mer's | day, ____ | ____ |
| B | The | stars be- | gin to | shine less | bright |
| C | And | slow - ly | fade a - | 6 . way. ____ | . ____ ‖ |

*H. H. Harbour*

TE ( 7̸ ) in Minor Mode
Mode of RE and Mode of LA Compared - Authentic Range

# Intonation

## Mode of RE and Mode of LA Compared - Authentic Range

TI and TE in Both Modes

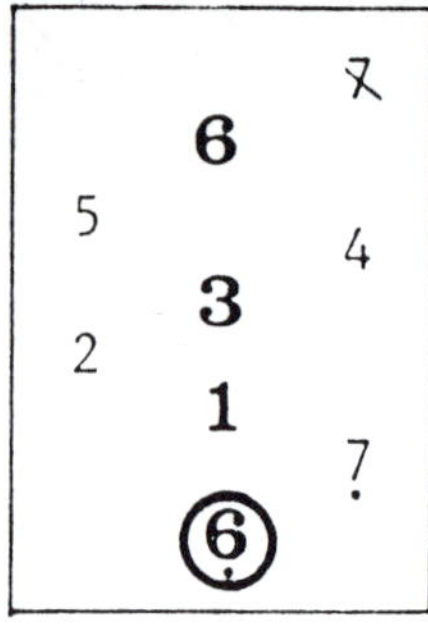


Intonation
Diagram 14

Intonation Exercise 18

| | |
|---|---|
| 5 | 1 |
| 4 | 7̸ |
| 3 | 6 |
| 2 | 5 |
| 1 | 4 |
| 7 | 3 |
| 6 | 2 |
| 5 | 1 |

Intonation
Diagram 16

Intonation Exercise 20 Sing on parallel columns

| 6 7 1 2 3 4 3 3 4 3 2 1 7 6 6 1 3 4 3 2 1 2 1 1 2 1 7 6 |
| 2 3 4 5 6 7̸ 6 6 7̸ 6 5 4 3 2 2 4 6 7̸ 6 5 4 5 4 4 5 4 3 2 |

| 3 4 3 2 3 . 6 . |
| 6 7̸ 6 5 6 . 2 . |

**Ear and Eye Tests**

# Rhythm

Review Rhythm and Metrical Gestures

| | |
|---|---|
| Rhythm Gesture IV | Binary, Ternary, Free for **HOLY SPIRIT** and ***KYRIE*** |
| Metrical Gesture III | for **SYON, AT THY SHINING GATES** |
| Metrical Gesture IV | for **JESUS, BREAD OF LIFE** |

# Notation

DO Clef on Line 5 of the Staff
Transcriptions
Sight-Singing Fragments

1. New Position of the DO Clef: Top Line of the Staff

When there is one flat in the key signature, the DO Clef is on the top line of the staff

Prepare for **COASTING SONG**

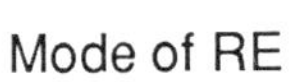

Prepare for Melody No. 21

2. Transcriptions

Staff to Number Notation

Number to Staff Notation

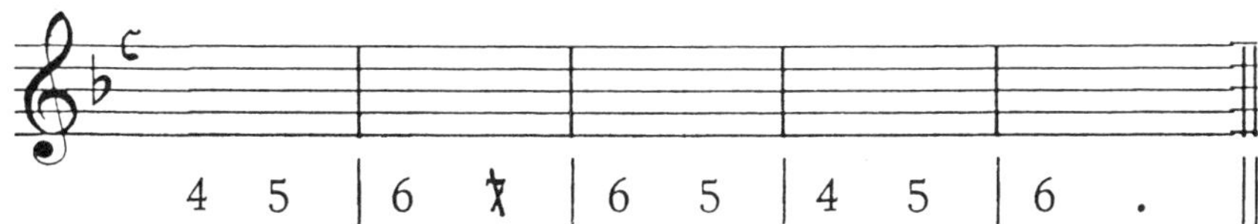


3. Sight-Singing Fragments

# Creative Activity

Song for Study of ABBC Form
Themes for Study and Improvisation

1. Review **GOOD MORNING, SIR SUNBEAM** Mode of SOL (from Book II)

| | | | | | |
|---|---|---|---|---|---|
| A | ‖ 5 | $\dot{1}$ . | 7 6 | 5 . | 5 |
| B | 5 | $\dot{1}$ . | 7 $\dot{1}$ | $\dot{2}$ . | 0 |
| B (b) | 5 | $\dot{1}$ . | 7 $\dot{1}$ | $\dot{2}$ . | $\dot{1}$ |
| C | 7 | 6 . | 7 6 | 5 . | . ‖ |

2. Theme for solution of ABBC or ABbC Form. Mode of DO

| | | | | |
|---|---|---|---|---|
| A | ‖ $\underset{\cdot}{5}$ | 1 . 2 . | 3 3 2 1 | 5 . . |
| B | | | | |
| B (b) | | | | |
| C | | | | ‖ |

3. Theme for solution of ABBC or ABbC Form. Mode of RE

Mode of RE Pentachord and Hexachord

# Intonation

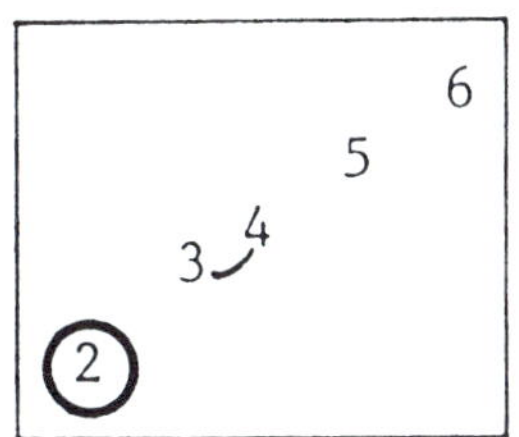


Intonation Diagram 17

a)

b)

Staff Diagrams 17

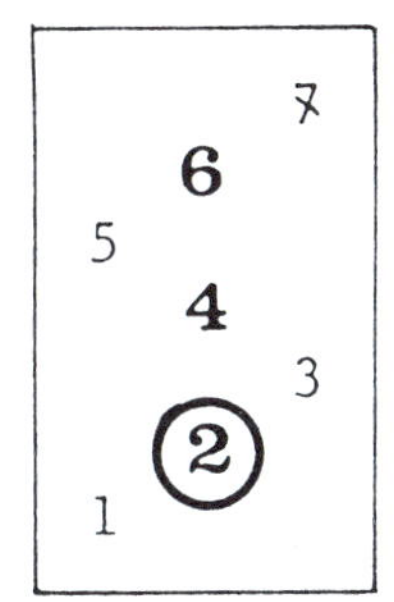


Intonation Diagram 18

a)

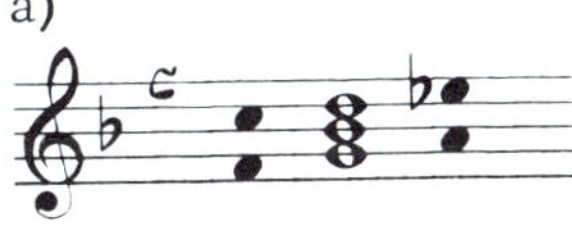

b)

Staff Diagrams 18

Intonation Exercise 21 Pentachord - Mode of RE

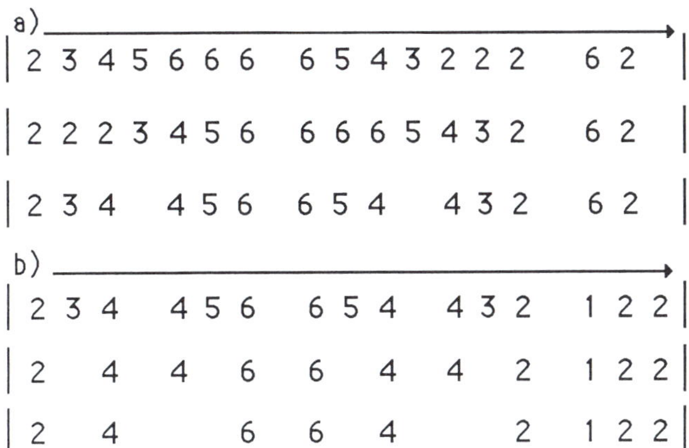

a)

| 2 3 4 5 6 6 6 | 6 5 4 3 2 2 2 | 6 2 |
|---|---|---|
| 2 2 2 3 4 5 6 | 6 6 6 5 4 3 2 | 6 2 |
| 2 3 4 4 5 6 | 6 5 4 4 3 2 | 6 2 |

b)

| 2 3 4 4 5 6 | 6 5 4 4 3 2 | 1 2 2 |
|---|---|---|
| 2 4 4 6 | 6 4 4 2 | 1 2 2 |
| 2 4 6 | 6 4 2 | 1 2 2 |

Intonation Exercise 22 Hexachord with 7̸

| 2 3 4 5 6 | 6 7̸ 6 | 6 5 4 3 2 |
|---|---|---|
| 2 4 6 | 6 7̸ 6 | 6 4 2 |
| 2 6 | 6 7̸ 6 | 6 2 |

**Ear and Eye Tests**

# Rhythm

Free Rhythm in RE Mode
Metrical Gestures in RE Mode
Begin Study of ***GLORIA IN EXCELSIS DEO*** Part I

1. Review Rhythm Gesture IV - Free, for Study of RE Mode Chants

   **MOST SACRED HEART OF JESUS** *(COR JESU SACRATISSIMUM)*

   **O SING UNTO THE LORD** *(CANTATE DOMINO)*

   ***KYRIE IX*** (First Kyrie)

2. Review Metrical Gestures with RE Mode Melodies

   Metrical Gesture III for Melody No. 22

   Metrical Gesture IV for **THANKSGIVING**

# Creative Activity

Dialogues in RE Mode
Compose Melody in RE Mode with Theme Given

Compose missing lines for the theme given in RE Mode in ABAb Form. The B Sections may be varied either melodically or rhythmically.

# Notation

Assimilation of Notation for RE Mode in Various Keys Studied
Transcription of ***COR JESU*** into Keys of:
C, E Flat, G, B Flat, D, F

Transcribe the chant given from Number Notation to Staff Notation in each of the keys given. Note the position of the DO Clef of each key.

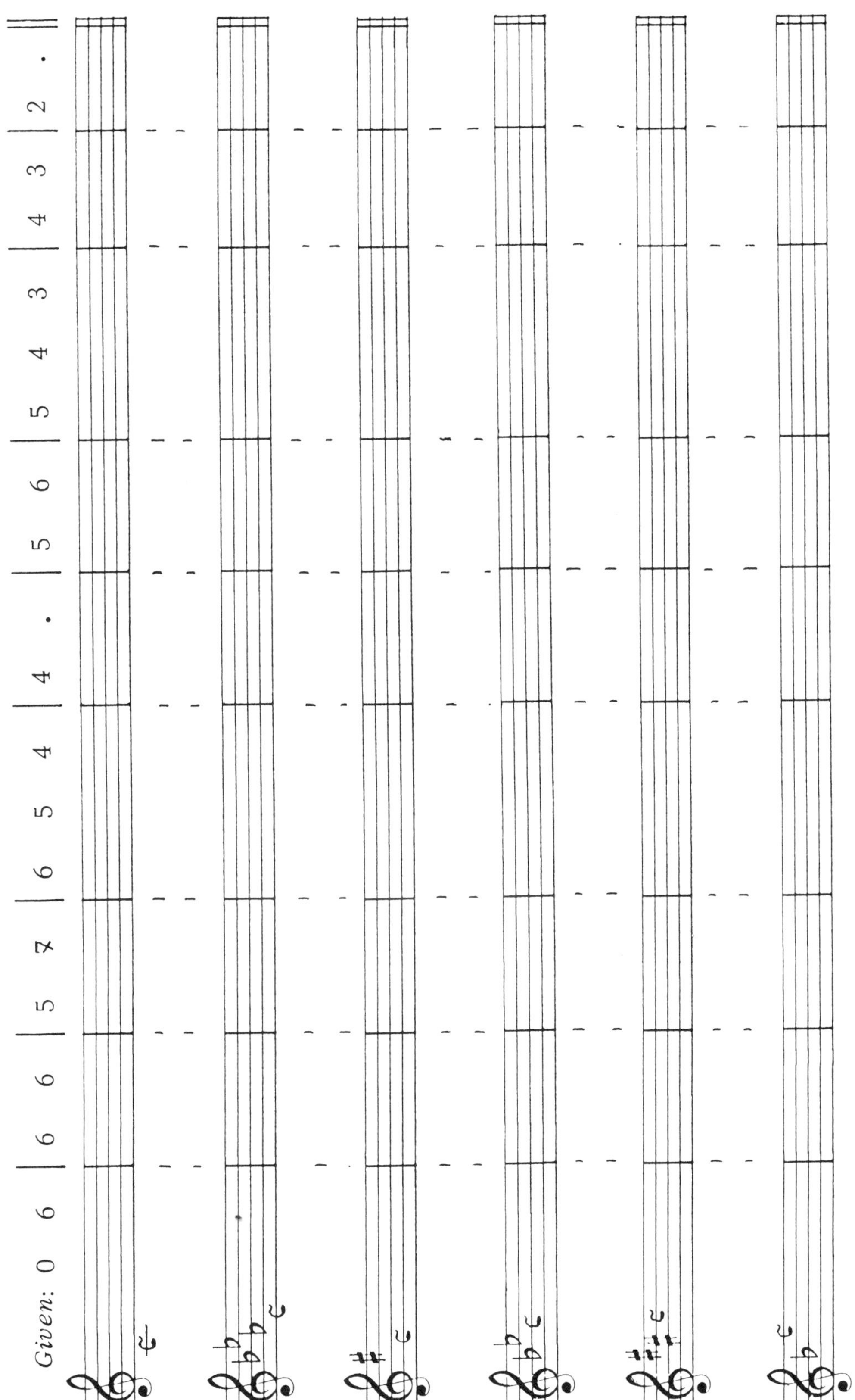

RE Mode Upper Tetrachord
Authentic Range 2 - 2̇
Use of both 7̶ and 7
Lower Tetrachord - Plagal Range 6̣ - 6

# Intonation

Authentic Range 2 - 2̇

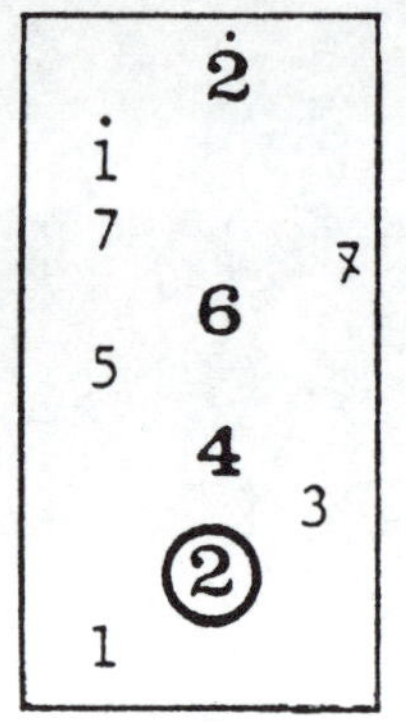


Intonation Diagram 19

Staff Diagram 19

**Ear and Eye Tests**

Plagal Range 6̣ - 6

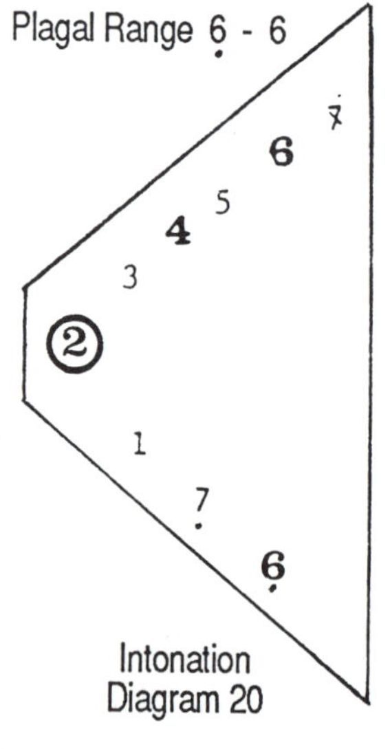


Intonation Diagram 20

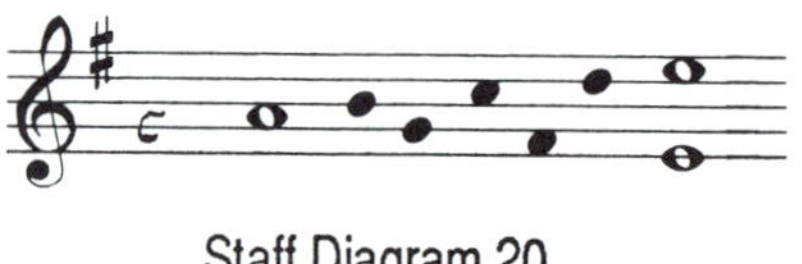

Staff Diagram 20

**Ear and Eye Tests**

# Rhythm

Derivation of Rhythm Patterns from Songs
Dictations

1. Derive Rhythm Patterns from songs of this chapter as dictated orally. Then say each pattern softly with Metrical Language and make appropriate gesture. Improvise a brief melody in RE Mode for each.

Rhythm Gesture III

a) **SEPTEMBER** Line 1

|| | | | | ||

|| | | | | ||

b) Melody No. 23 Line 1

|| | | | | ||

|| | | | | ||

Metrical Gesture II

a) **THE VIOLIN** Line 1

|| | | | ||

|| | | | ||

b) **NEAR GENTLE OX AND ASS HE LIES** Line 2

|| | | | ||

|| | | | ||

2. Dictations

Derive rhythm from the spoken line taken from **THE VIOLIN**

"With a bow and string it can sweetly sing."

Derive rhythm from the spoken line taken from **SEPTEMBER**

"With fruit are bending down."

Derive rhythm from the spoken line taken from **GOD REST YE MERRY, GENTLEMEN**

"O tidings of comfort and joy, comfort and joy!"

# Notation

RE Mode with Key Signature of Two Sharps
Transcriptions

1. Transcribe to Number Notation the last two lines of **SEPTEMBER**

2. Transcribe to Staff Notation the first two lines of **NEAR GENTLE OX AND ASS HE LIES**

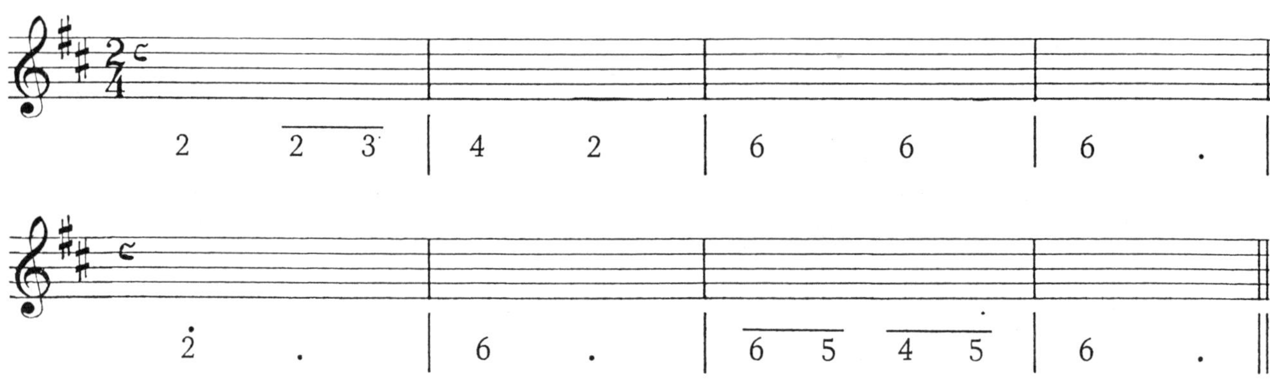


3. Transcribe to Staff Notation

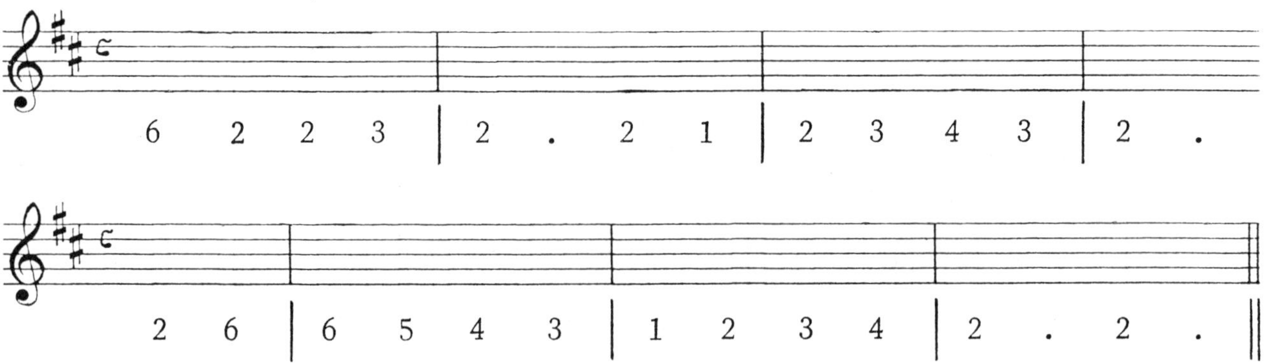

# Creative Activity

Continuing Study of Forms: AAbB, AAbA, AABb,
Composition Exercise in RE Mode With and Without Words

Compose a Melody in DO Mode with Theme A Given in ABbA Form

Compose a Melody in Mode of RE with Text Given
Binary or Ternary Rhythm
Melodic Form to be Chosen by Student

| | | | | |
|---|---|---|---|---|
| *Verse 1* | Pi - ping | down the | val - leys | wild, |
| | Pi - ping | songs of | plea - sant | glee, |
| | On a | cloud I | saw a | child, |
| | And he | laugh - ing | said to | me, |
| *Verse 2* | "Pipe a | song a - | bout a | Lamb!" |
| | So I | piped with | mer - ry | cheer, |
| | "Pi - per, | pipe that | song a - | gain!" |
| | So I | piped; he | wept to | hear. |

*William Blake*
*"Songs of Innocence"*

The Third Accidental FA#, FI (Fee)

# Intonation

**Ear and Eye Tests**

FI in the Major Pentachord

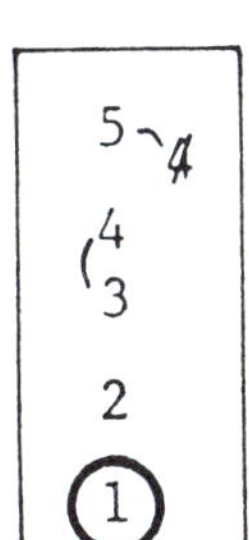


Intonation Diagram 21

Staff Diagram 21

a)

b)

c)

d)

FI in the Major Tetrachord

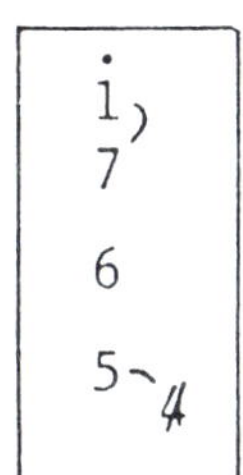


Intonation Diagram 22

Staff Diagram 22

a)

b)

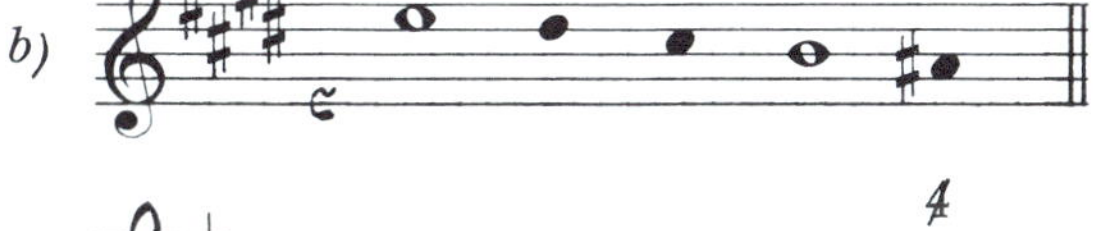

c)

## Rhythm

Compound Duple Time in Ternary Groups
Within Larger Binary Rhythm
Review Rhythm Gesture II, Metrical Gestures I and II
Metrical Language

Rhythm Patterns **Series 10** with Rhythm Gesture II or Metrical Gesture II

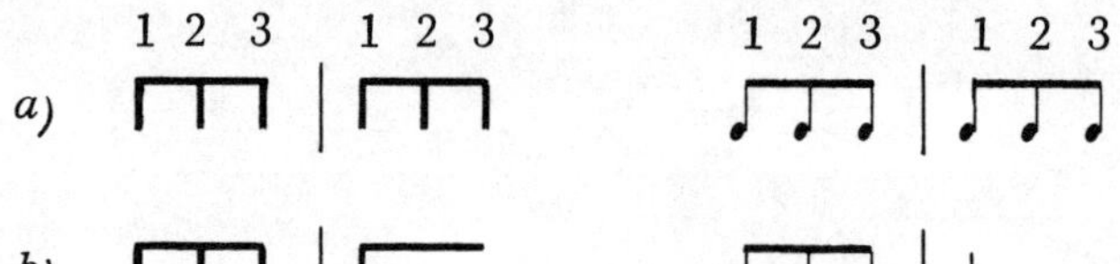


**Rhythmic Dictations**

## Notation

Time Signatures for Compound Duple Time
Continue Study of Accidentals:
Flat ♭
Sharp ♯
Cancel ♮
Transcriptions

Transcriptions

Transcribe to Staff Notation:

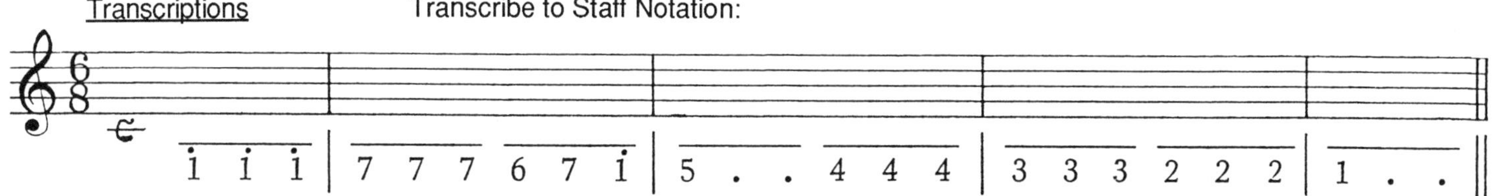


Transcribe the following from Number to Staff Notation:

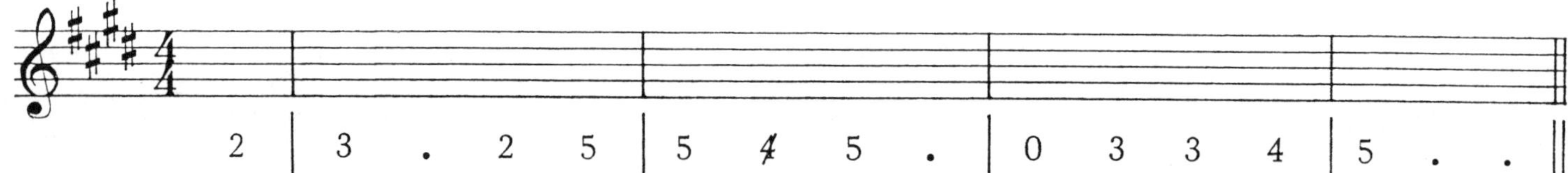


Transcribe the following from Staff to Number Notation:

# Creative Activity

Improvisations on New Rhythm Patterns

1. Combinations of Rhythm Patterns Series 10

Combinations of rhythm patterns can provide new rhythmic bases for melodies in Mode of DO. Improvise a theme for each of the following rhythms:

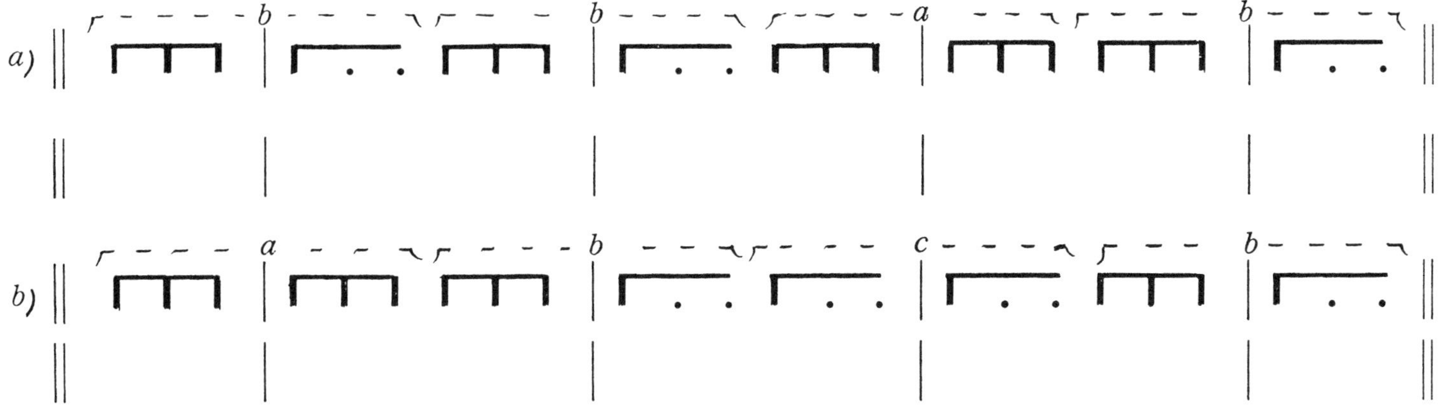


2. Compose a Melody to Given Text: Mode of DO; 4; 6/8 Time

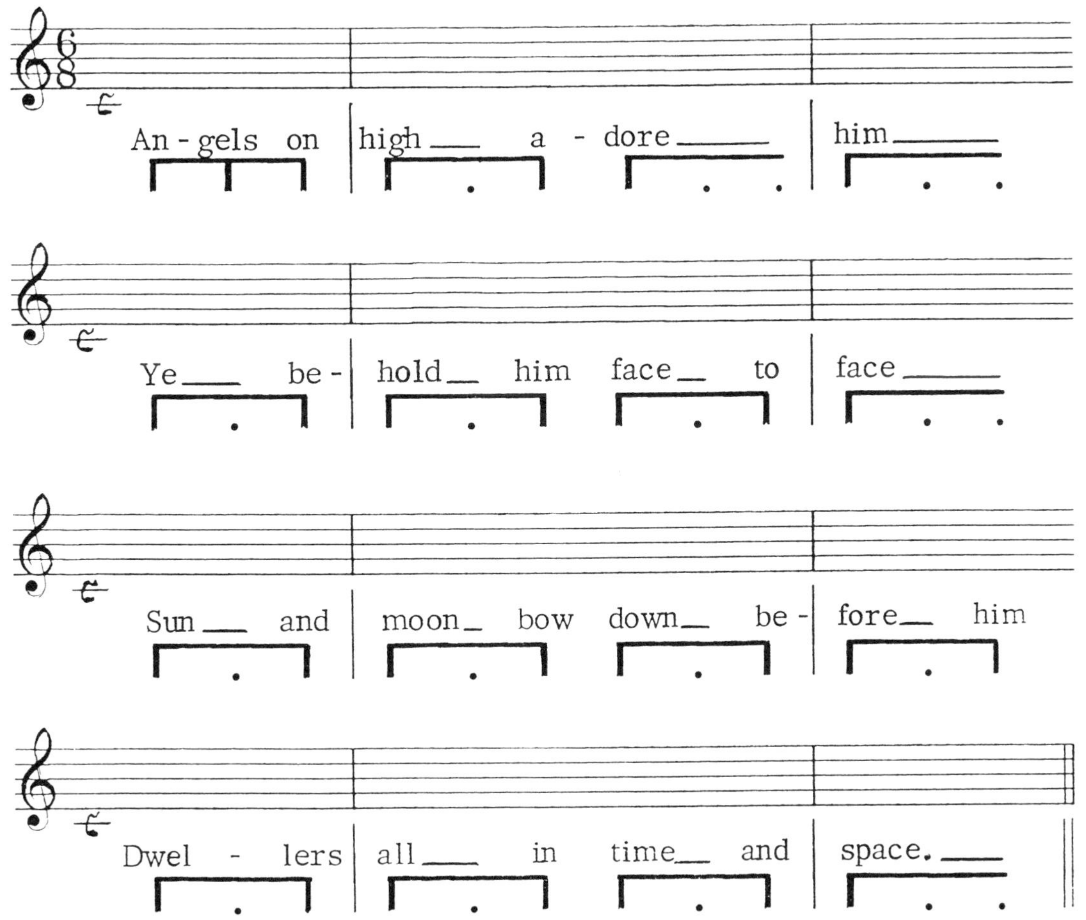


Lines form Psalm 103 paraphrase by H. F. Lyte

Study of FA# 4 (FI) Continued

# Intonation

Intonation Diagram 21

Staff Diagram 21e

1̇
2̇
7
6
5
4
4
3
2
1

Intonation Diagram 24

Staff Diagram 24

**Ear and Eye Tests**

# Rhythm

6/8 Time with Rhythm Gesture II Continued

Rhythm Patterns **Series 10** - Extended

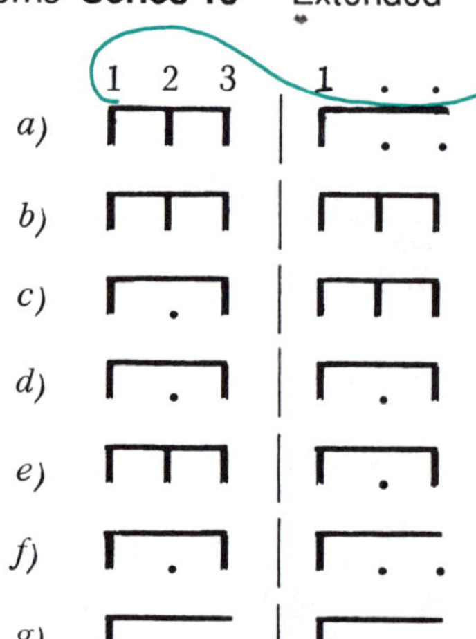

Rhythmic Dictations on next page

**Rhythmic Dictations**

# Notation

Transcribing FA# 4̸ in the keys of G, D, and E Flat

1. From Staff Notation to Number Notation

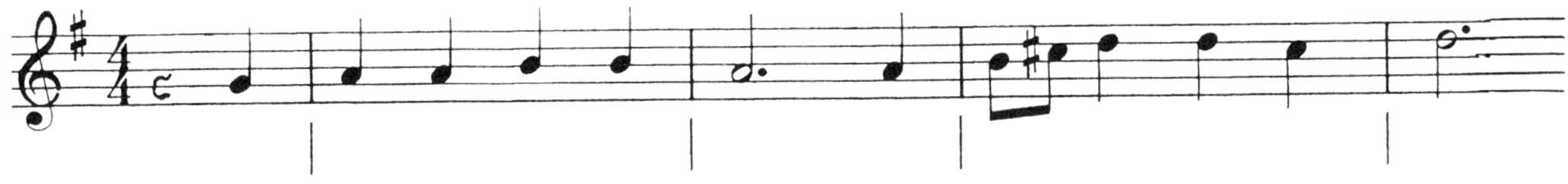

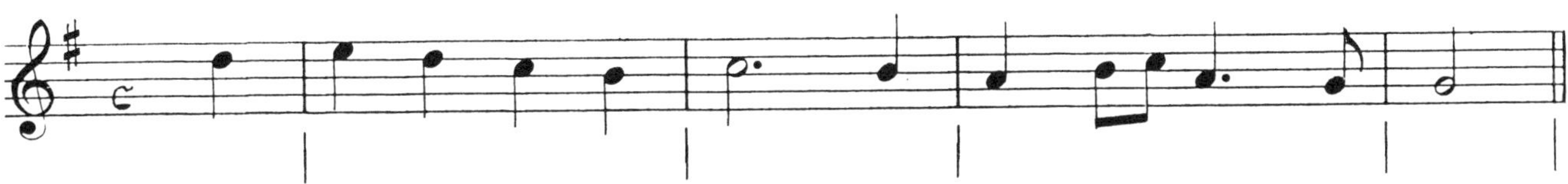

2. From Number Notation to Staff Notation

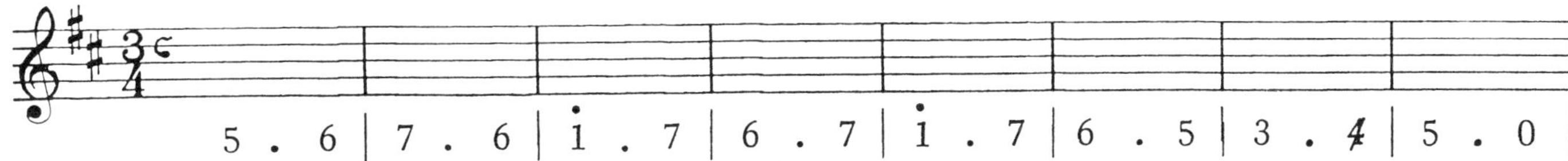


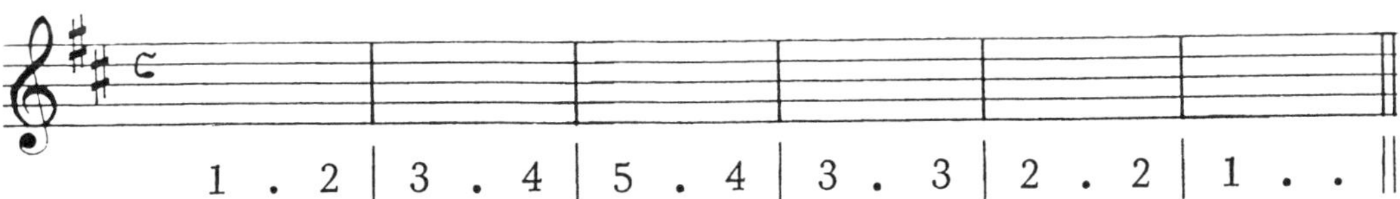


3. From Staff Notation to Number Notation

# Creative Activity

Questions and Answers in 6/8 Time
Composing a Melody for a Given Text

1. Questions and answers in 6/8 Time

Step 1: Student asks the question and sings a possible answer, repeating the action until all suggested answers have been sung.

Step 2: Student places a hand over the answers, asks the question and improvises an answer.

Possible Answers

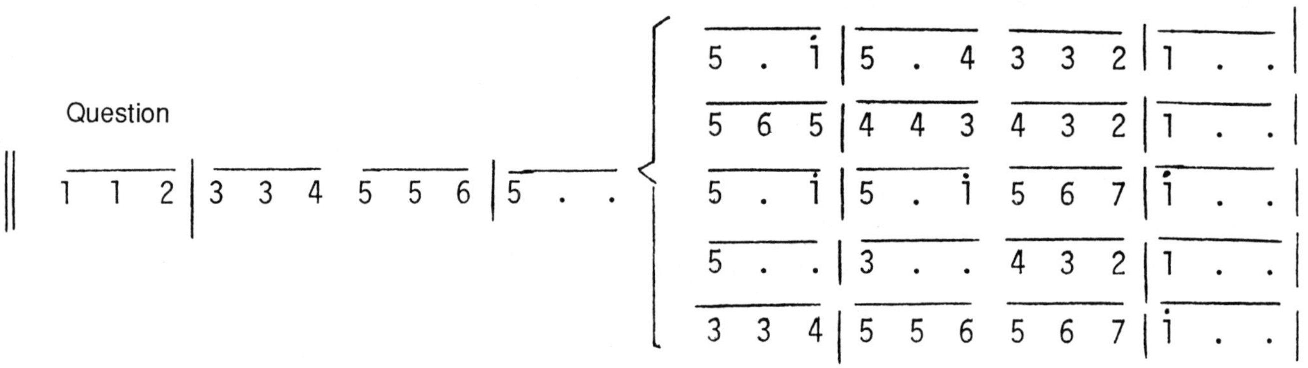

```
Question                                {  5 . 1̇ | 5 . 4   3 3 2 | 1 . . |
                                           5 6 5 | 4 4 3   4 3 2 | 1 . . |
|| 1 1 2 | 3 3 4   5 5 6 | 5 . .          5 . 1̇ | 5 . 1̇   5 6 7 | 1̇ . . |
                                           5 . . | 3 . .   4 3 2 | 1 . . |
                                           3 3 4 | 5 5 6   5 6 7 | 1̇ . . |
```

2. Compose a Melody for a Given Text

|| Go to bed | first,__ a gold - en | purse;

Go to bed | sec - ond, a gold - en | pheas-ant;

Go to bed | third,__ a gold - en | bird. ||

*Anonymous Jingle*

# Lesson 15

# Intonation

Approaching FA# 4̸ by a Skip

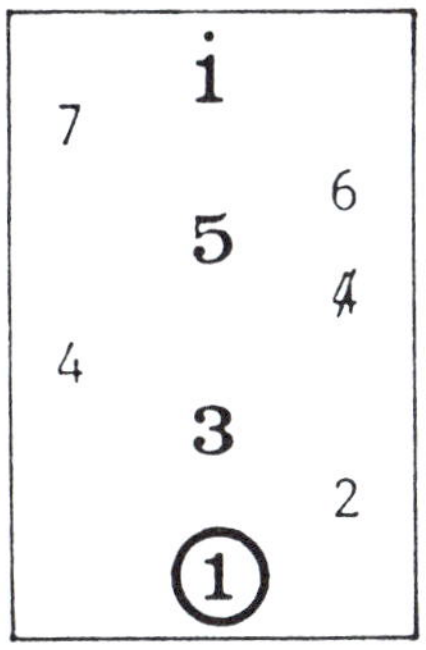

1̇
7
6
5
4̸
4
3
2
①

Intonation Diagram 25

Intonation Exercise 30 6 4̸ and 4̸ 6 in upper tetrachord

| 1̇ 5 6 6 5 4̸ 5 5 4̸ 5 6 6 5 1̇ |
| 1̇ 6 6 [5] 4̸ 5 5 4̸ [5] 6 6 5 1̇ |
| 1̇ 6 [5] 4̸ 5 [5] 4̸ [5] 6 5 1̇ |

Intonation Exercise 31 4̸ 6 and 6 4̸ in the hexachord

| 1 3 5 5 4̸ 5 6 6 5 4̸ 5 5 3 1 |
| 1 3 5 5 4̸ [5] 6 6 [5] 4̸ 5 5 3 1 |
| 1 3 5 4̸ [5] 6 6 [5] 4̸ [5] 5 3 1 |

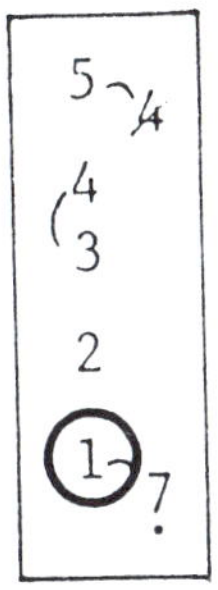

5 4̸
4 3
2
① 7̣

Intonation Diagram 26

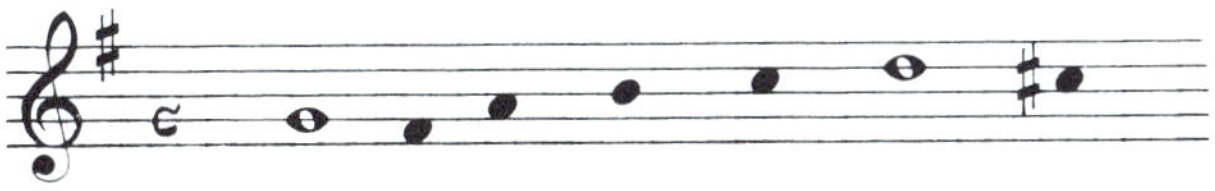

Staff Diagram 26

Intonation Exercise 32

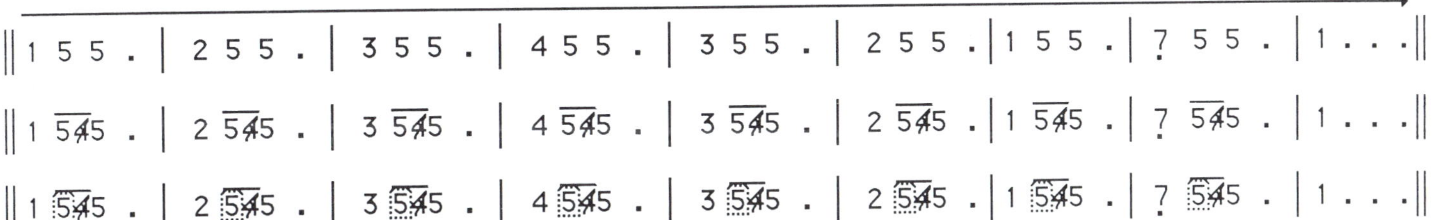


Practice this exercise in strict time - not too fast. "Think" tones in strict time.

**Ear and Eye Tests**

# Rhythm

6/8 Compound Duple Time (Continued) with Rhythm Gesture II

Rhythm Patterns **Series 11** Extension of Series 10

Say rhythm with Metrical Gesture I and Metrical Language

Sing Rhythm on notes given with Metrical Gesture II

Improvise melodies on Rhythm Patterns, singly and in combination

**Dictations**

# Notation

Transcriptions
Sight-Singing Drills

1. Transcribe to Number Notation

2. Transcribe to Staff Notation

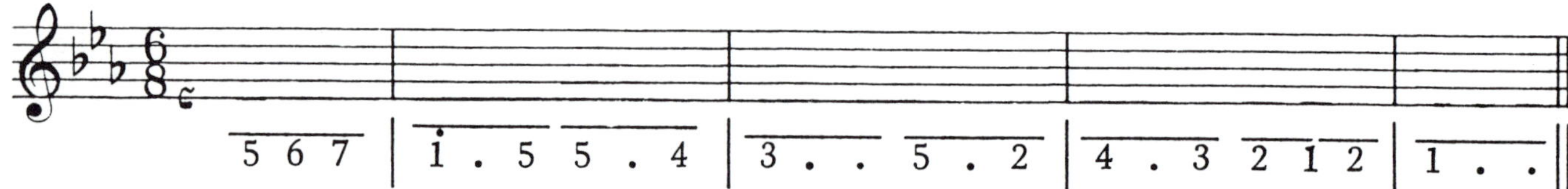

3. Sight-Singing Drills with intervals taken from Intonation Exercises
   Repeat each exercise several times

## Creative Activity

Composition in ABCA Form Based on Rhythm Patterns in Compound Duple Time
Mode of DO

The lines to be composed may vary melodically and/or rhythmically from line A.
Neither of these two lines should end on DO.

# Intonation

FA# ( 4 ) in Minor Mode - Plagal Range
RE Mode - Plagal Range

1. LA Mode with FA# ( 4 ) in upper Tetrachord

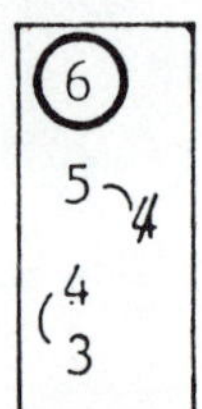


Intonation Diagram 27

Staff Diagrams 27a and 27b

**Ear and Eye Tests**

2. Minor Tetrachord with FA# ( 4 ) extended downward is the same as RE Mode

To hear the similarity of the two modes, sing each column several times

**Ear and Eye Tests**

| | |
|---|---|
| 6 | 2 |
| 5 | 1 |
| 4 | 7 |
| 3 | 6 |
| 2 | 5 |
| 1 | 4 |
| 7 | 3 |
| (6) | (2) |
| 5 | 1 |

Intonation Diagram 28a

3. Plagal Range of RE Mode sounds the same as LA Mode with FA# ( 4 )

**Ear and Eye Tests**

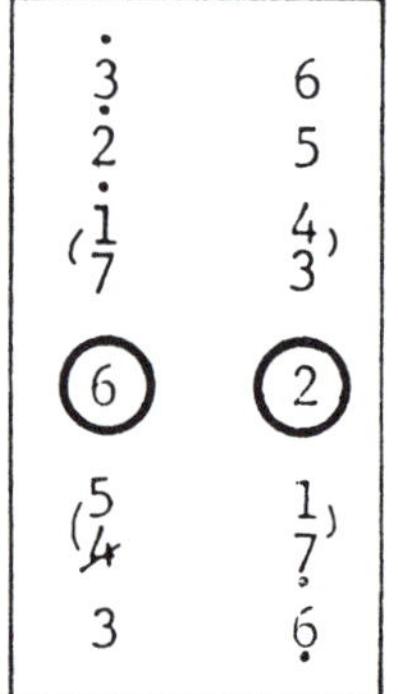


Intonation Diagram 28b

# Rhythm

6/8 Compound Time Continued
Tied Notes over the Middle of a Measure

Rhythm Patterns **Series 12**

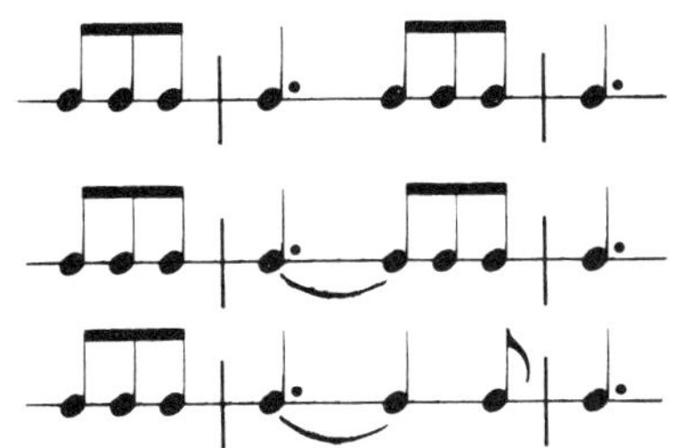

The tied note in the middle of the measure occurs frequently in melodies in 6/8 time. Careful preparation of the rhythmic patterns of each song will have good results.

Practice with Metrical Gesture I and Metrical Language

Sing each rhythm on tones given with Rhythm Gesture II or Metrical Gesture II

Combine patterns for improvisations and dictations

**Dictations**

# Notation

Alternate Ways of Writing Melodies in RE Mode
Transcribing Melodies in Compound Duple Time
Sight-Singing Drills with FA# ( 4 )

1. Transcribe RE Mode melody to LA Mode. Use Number and Staff Notation.

2. Transcribe a fragment of **HIGH BARBARY** to Number Notation

# Creative Activity

Improvise Melodies in 6/8 Time
ABAC Form in DO Mode
Compose Melody for Given Text

1. Improvise a melody with A theme given. The form is ABAC.

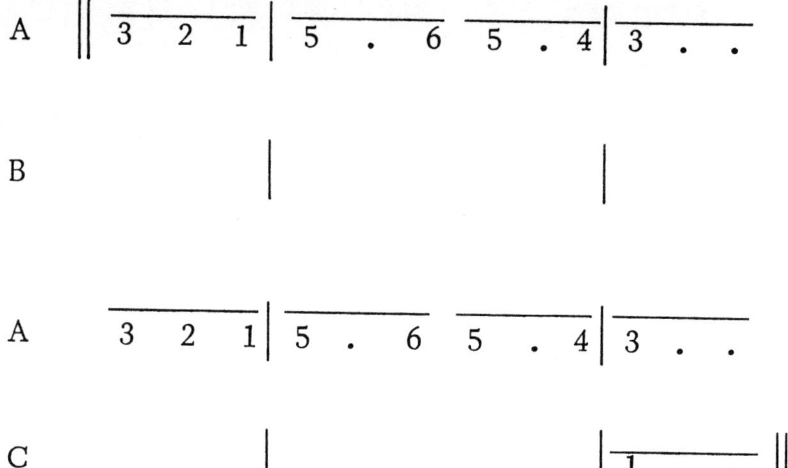


2. Compose a melody in LA Mode with 𝅘𝅥. and given text.

A. L. Waring

Study of Plagal Ranges of LA Mode with FA# ( ) and RE Mode Continued

# Intonation

Intonation Exercise to prepare for Melody No. 34

1. Sing note-names of exercises in Lines 1, 2, and 3
2. Sing note-names of song in line 4

LA Mode with FA# ( )

Repeat steps 1 and 2 for the following exercises
Notice the similarity of sound with the version given above.

RE Mode

# Rhythm

Presentation of 3/2 Time

Rhythm Patterns **Series 13**

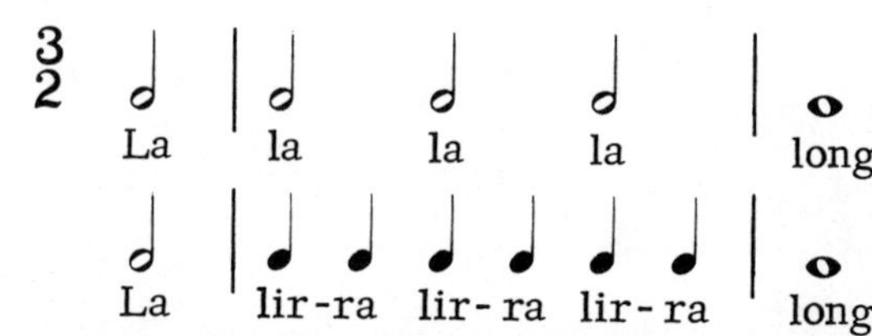


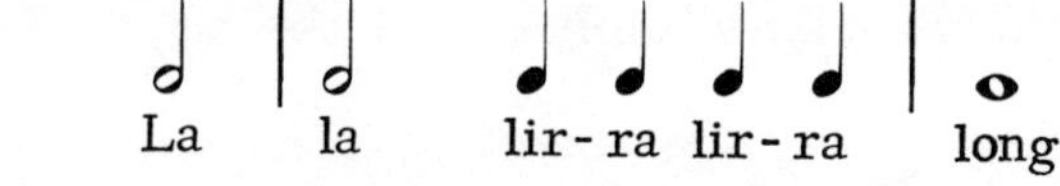

**Metrical Gesture III** is used with this melody and rhythm:

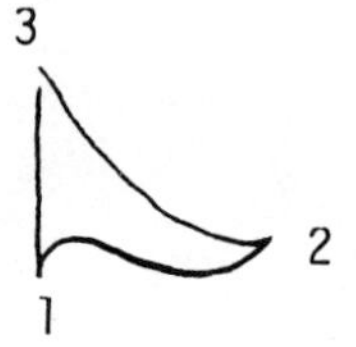


**THE CLOUDS OF NIGHT ARE PASSED AWAY**

Continue writing Metrical Language beneath the Staff Notation melody

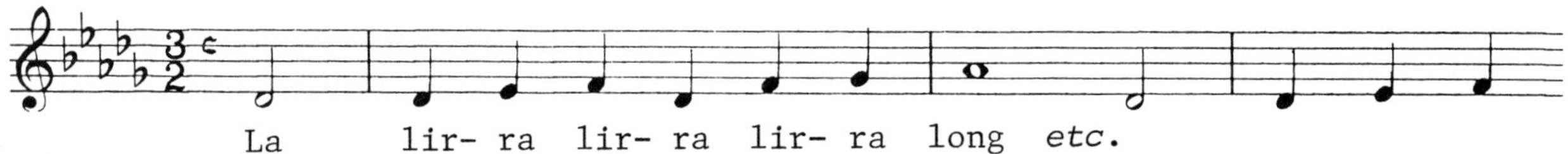

# Notation

DO Clef on Line 4 in Key of Five Flats
Transcriptions
3/2 Time Signature

1. DO Clef on Line 4

This position of the DO Clef has already been seen in the key of two sharps.

Transcribe the following from Number Notation to Staff Notation

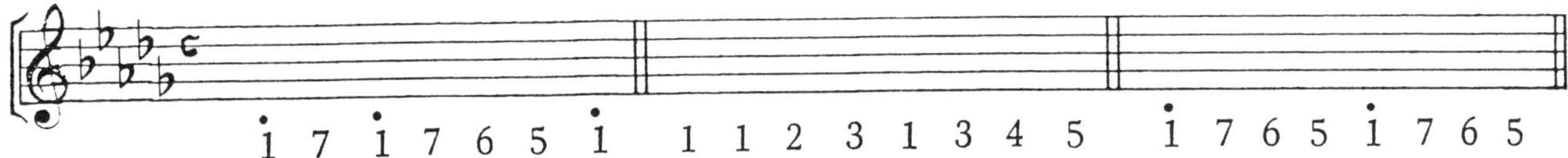

2. Transcribe the following rhythms to Staff Notation

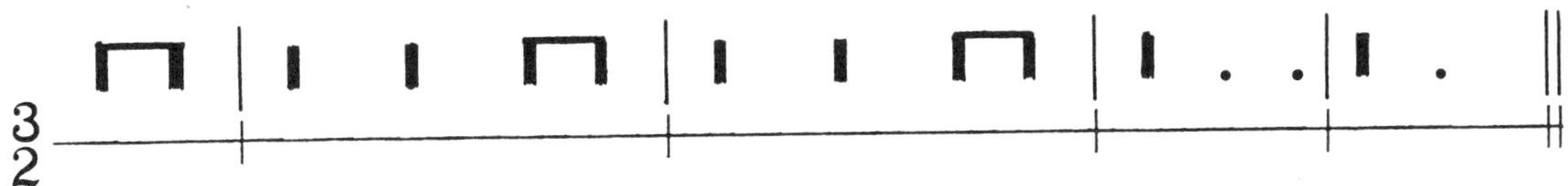

3. Transcribe the following to Number Notation

4. Example shown is in 6/8 Time. Transcribe to 3/2 Time. In the first example, the eighth-note ♪ is the unit of the pulse. In the second example, the half-note 𝅗𝅥 is the unit of the pulse.

# Creative Activity

Composition with Words and Dynamics
Improvise Responses in 3/2 Time

1. Provide a melodic design in ABAC Form for the given text. Include marks of dynamics. RE Mode, Plagal Range.

A Let us now with glad - some mind

B Praise the Lord for he is kind;

A For his mer - cies still en - dure,

C Ev - er faith - ful, ev - er sure.

*Old English Hymn*

Suggested procedure:
1. Read text aloud
2. Mark verbal stresses
3. Determine rhythm
4. Add melodic design

2. Compose a response in 3/2 Time to the statement given below. DO Mode.

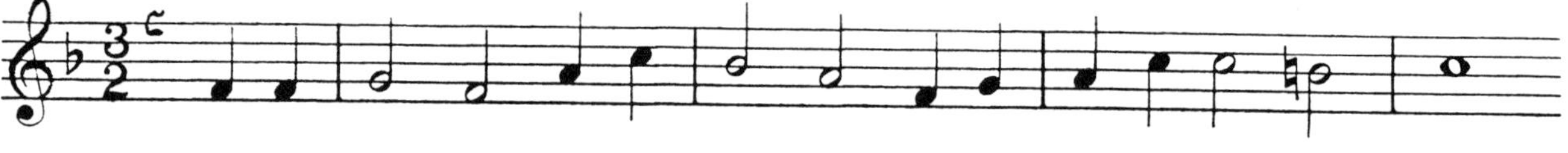

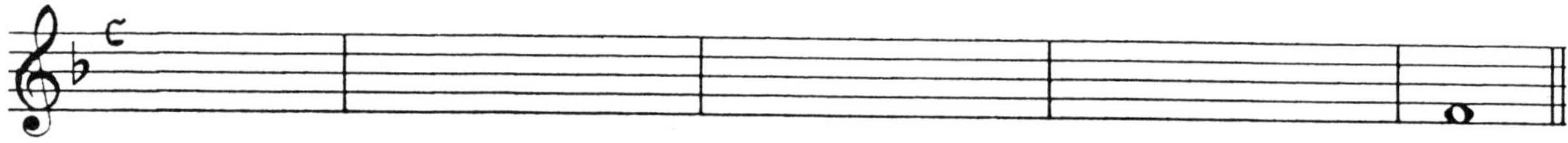

The rhythm of the response may be the same as that of the statement but the pitches must be different. End on DO.

**Dictations**

The Accidental DO# - DI (Dee - ɣ )

# Intonation

## Intonation Exercises and Dictations

### DO# ( ɣ ) in the RE Pentachord

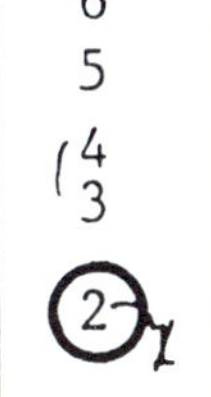


Intonation Diagram 29

See Melody No. 36

### DO# ( ɣ ) in LA Hexachord

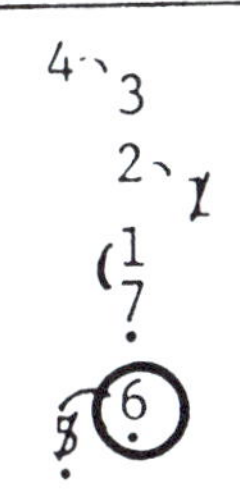


Intonation Diagram 30

See Melody No. 35 and line 3 of
**I CLASP UNTO MY HEART THIS DAY**

### DO# ( ɣ ) in DO Pentachord

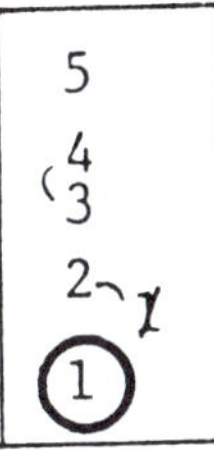


Intonation Diagram 31

see **CALINO CUSTURAME**
and **AMERICA, THE BEAUTIFUL**

# Rhythm

Syncopation in 3/4 and 4/4 Time
Ties Across the Bar Line

1. Syncopation in 3/4 and 4/4 Time

A syncopation occurs when the long note of the melody is heard on the weak pulse of the measure. For example:

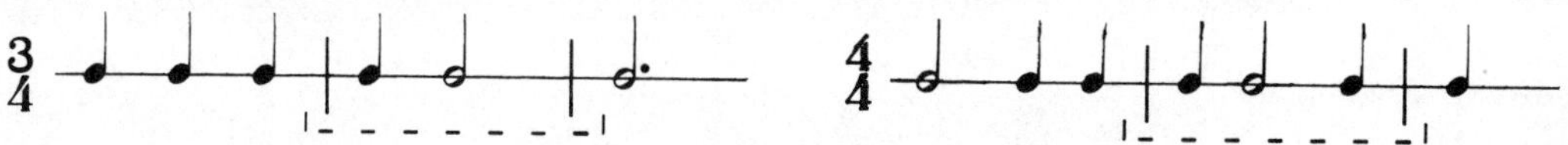

This shift of the long note from the first to the second pulse of the measure momentarily disturbs the feeling of regularity which metrical rhythms normally achieve.

See last line of **LITTLE LAMB, WHO MADE THEE?** 3/4 Time

See first line of **BE THOU MY VISION** 4/4 Time

2. Ties across the Bar Line

Ties across the bar line were studied in Books I and II. These ties involved notes of even pulse values. For example:

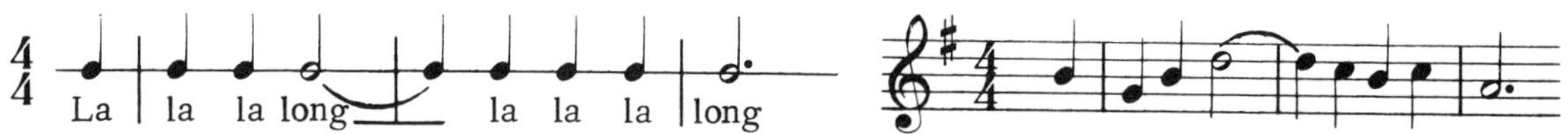


In this lesson the long note tied to a note, or notes, <u>of half-pulse values</u> is seen for the first time. For example:

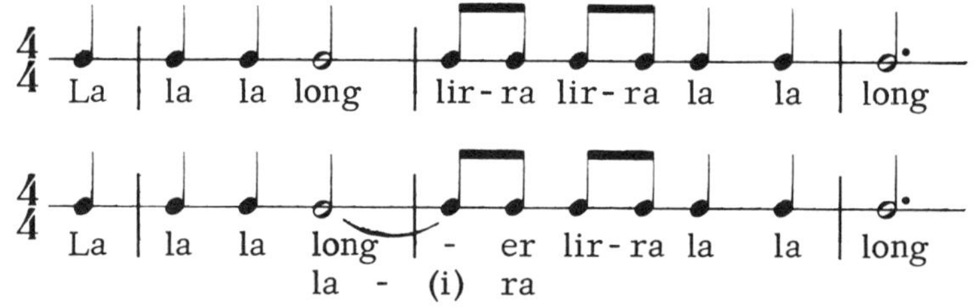


Practice the following with Metrical Gestures I and IV

# Creative Activity

Composing in 6/8 Time with "A" Theme Given

Complete the melody shown below. Use DO Mode with DO#

# Notation

Finding Place of DO from Key Signature - Review

Place the DO Clef on the correct line for each of the following key signatures:
(Remember the jingle: "If sharps you see, the last is TI. If flats there are, the last is FA.")

N.B. The placement of the DO Clef on the line above the staff, as in the keys of A and AFlat, will be discussed in following lessons.

Crossing Tonal Bridges between the Major and Relative Minor Modes in the Pentachord Ranges

# Intonation

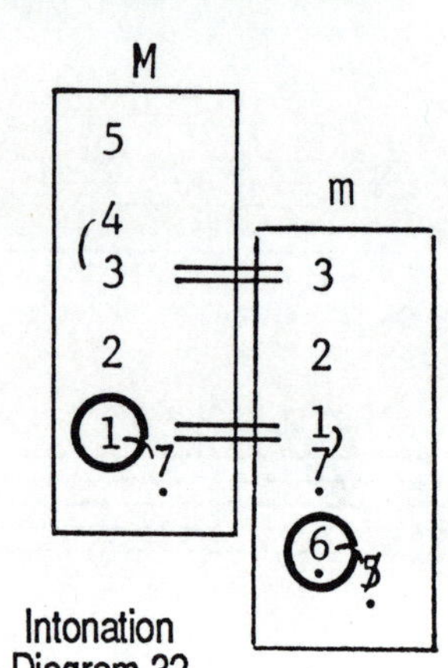


Intonation Diagram 32

Staff Diagram 32

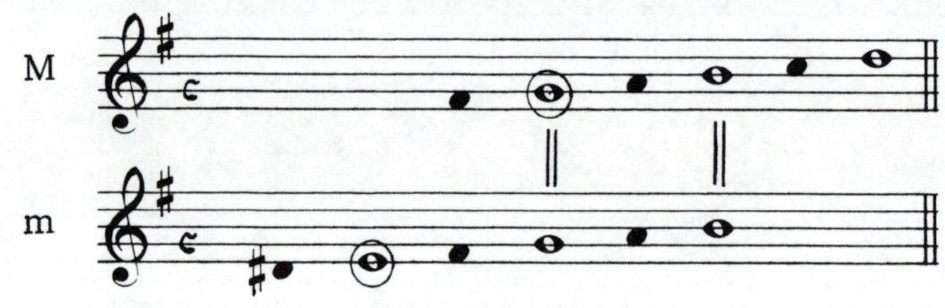


Intonation Exercise 38

M (Major) — bridge — m (minor)

‖ 1 2 3 4 5 4 3 2 1 7 1 2 3 . . == 3 2 1 7 6 5 6 7 1 2 3 2 3 . . ‖

‖ 3 4 5 4 3 2 1 2 3 2 1 7 1 . . == 1 7 6 5 6 7 6 7 1 2 3 2 1 . . ‖

Intonation Exercise 39 Crossing the tonal "bridges" of a melody

a) ‖ (m) 6 7 1 2 | 3 . 1 7 | 6 . 1 0 | == | (M) 1 2 3 4 | 5 . 3 2 | 1 . . 0 |

| 5 4 3 2 | 1 . 7 1 | 2 . 3 . | == | (m) 3 2 1 7 | 6 . 5 7 | 6 . . 0 ‖

b) ‖ (m) 6 6 3 3 | 2 3 1 . | == | (M) 1 1 5 5 | 3 4 2 . |

| 2 4 3 2 | 1 2 3 . | == | (m) 3 6 7 2 | 1 7 6 . ‖

Now study **SHEPHERDS IN THE FIELDS ABIDING** and Melody No. 37

**Ear and Eye Tests**

# Rhythm

Compound Duple Rhythm 6/8 Beginning on a Down-Pulse

Rhythm Patterns **Series 14** - Metrical Gesture II

Preparatory Exercises

Notice the tie in d)

First practice preparatory exercises with Metrical Language and Metrical Gesture II
Notice that ♩. ♩. = 𝅗𝅥.

Sing the remaining lines on the neutral syllable Du while maintaining a steady pulse.
Repeat each line several times before going on to the next.

**Dictations**

# Notation

DO Clef on Line Above the Staff

Authentic and Plagal Ranges

1. Transcribe to Staff Notation:

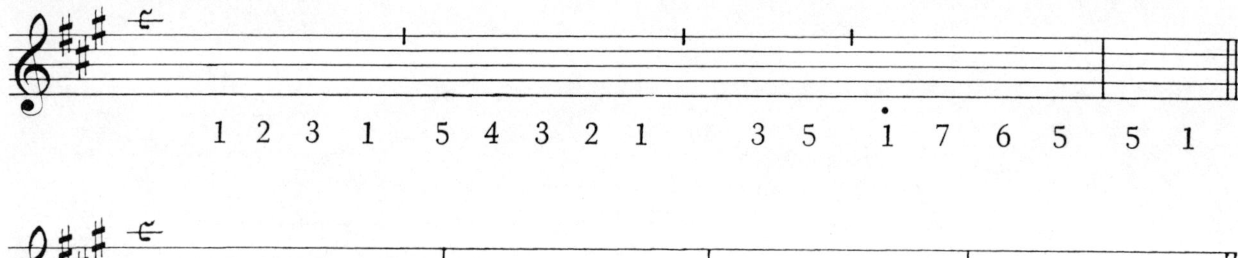


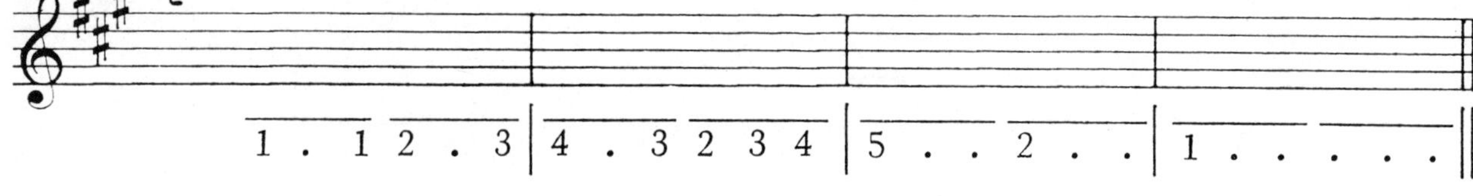


2. Transcribe to Number Notation:

3. Preparatory Exercise for **HEAVE AWAY**

Repeat each segment several times on note names

# Creative Activity

Compose Two Answering Lines to Themes Proposed
Improvise on Intonation Diagram 32
Compose a Melody for Given Text Including a Modulation from Major to Minor Modes

1. Compose a melody for lines 3 and 4 of the following. The resulting form may be ABAC or ABCa

2. Improvise on the two columns of Intonation Diagram 32. Make use of the "bridges"

3. Provide a melody for the given text. Include a modulation to the Relative Minor

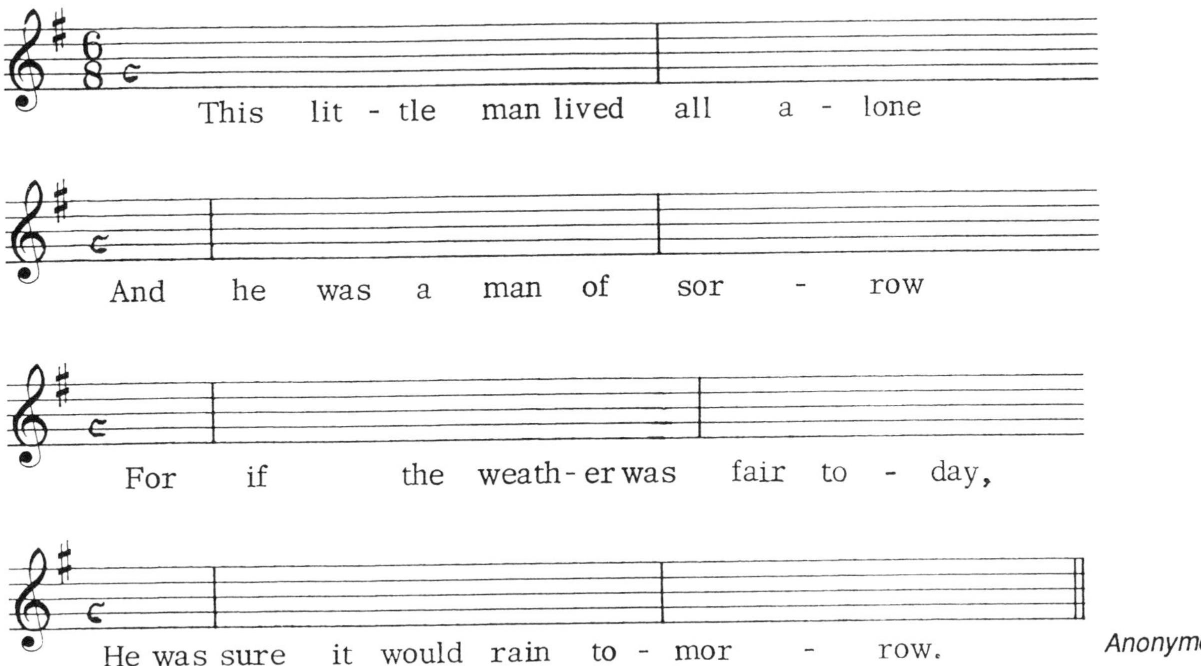


*Anonymous*

Crossing Bridges Between Major and Minor Modes - Continued
DO Mode - Plagal Range
LA Mode - Authentic Range

# Intonation

6 | 6
5 | 5
4 3 | 4 3
2 | 2
1 7 | 1 7
6 | 6
5 | 5

Intonation Diagram 33

Staff Diagram 33 see **DOWN THE RIVER**

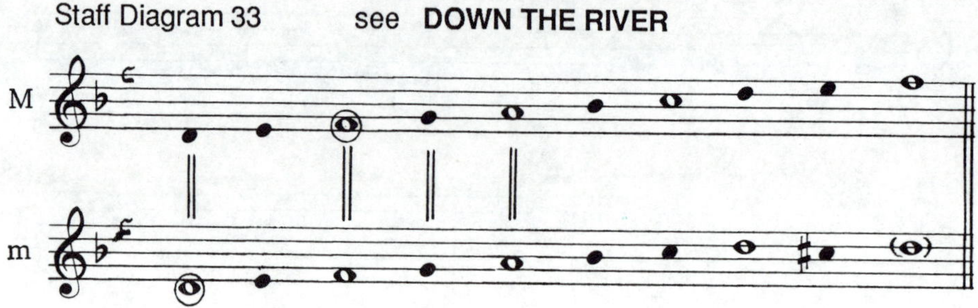


Intonation Exercise 40

Practice one line of the exercise at a time. Then sing the entire exercise without stopping, going back and forth from one column or music line to the next.

*Notice the four "bridges" where shifts in the mode can be made*

see Melody No. 39

| M 1 5 1 3 5 4 3 . ═ m 3 4 3 6 6 6̸ 6 . 3 . ═
| M 3 4 5 4 3 2 1 . ═ m 1 2 1 7 6 6̸ 6 . ═
| M 6 5 1 2 3 4 2 . ═ m 2 4 3 2 1 7 6 . ═
| 6 6̸ 6 3 2 4 3 ═ M 3 5 3 2 4 3 1 . ═

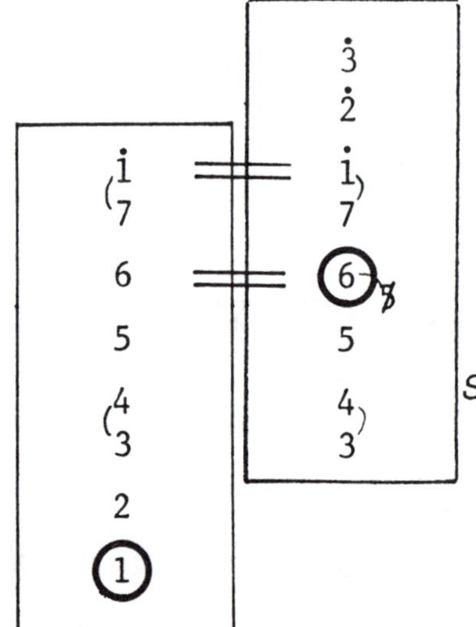


Intonation Diagram 34

Intonation Exercise 41

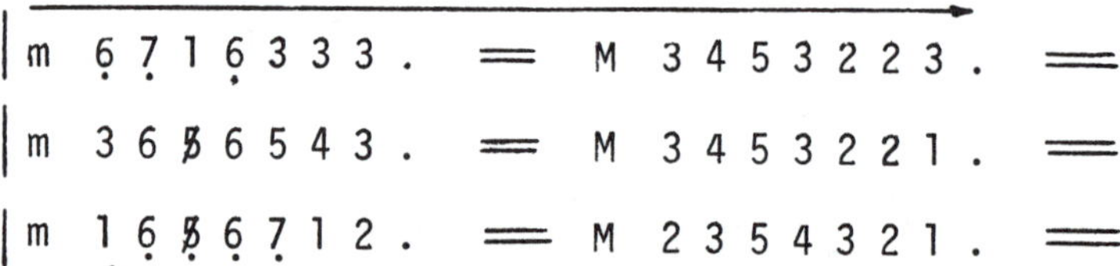


*Special diagram for study of* Melody No. 40

**Ear and Eye Tests**

# Rhythm

Compound Duple Time 6/8 Beginning on Down-Pulse - Continued
Feminine Endings

Rhythm Patterns **Series 15**

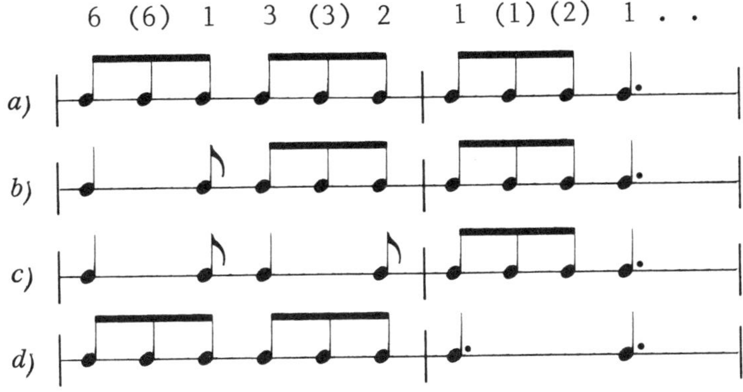


*The "Feminine Ending" is present when the long note at the end of a phrase occurs on the up-pulse of the measure*

Practice the rhythms here as in Lesson 19, first with Metrical Gesture I and the neutral syllable "Du."
Then change to Metrical Gesture II and sing the rhythms on the melody suggested above.

See **IF YOU WOULD HEAR THE ANGELS SING**
and **POP, GOES THE WEASEL**

**Improvisations and Dictations**

# Notation

DO Clef on the Line Above the Staff: Key of Four Flats
Summary of Staff Notation Rests

Authentic and Plagal Range

1. Transcribe to Staff Notation:

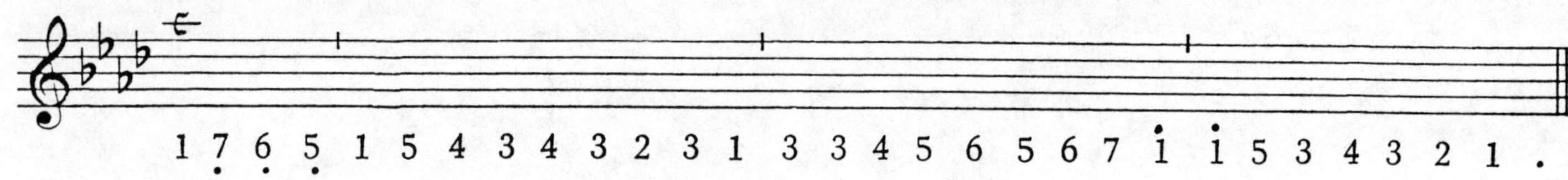


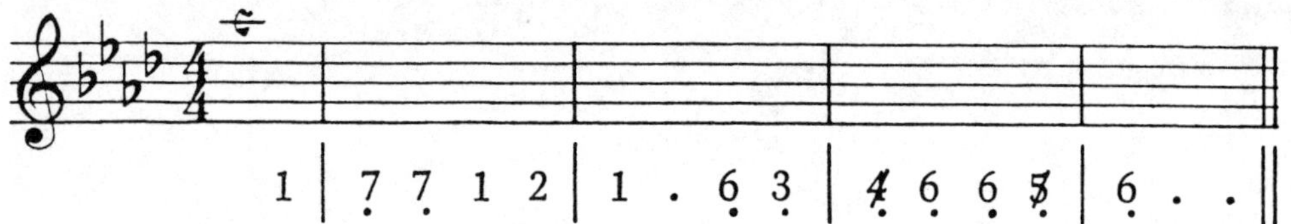


2. Transcribe to Number Notation:

3. Summary of Staff Notation Rests

*For every note in* Staff Notation *there is an equivalent rest. For example:*

Transcribe on the lower staff the equivalent rest values of the notes given.

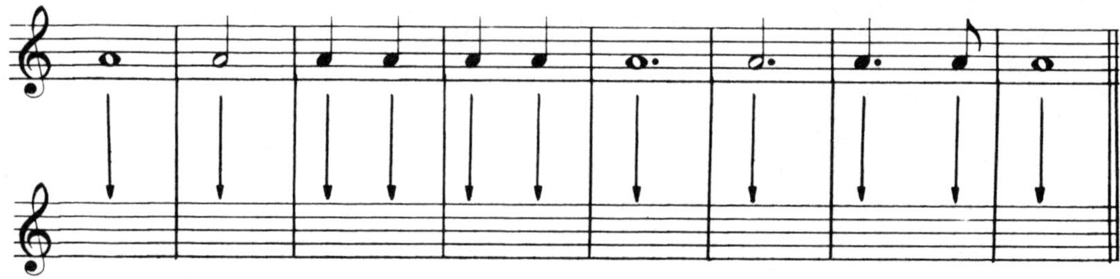

# Creative Activity

Composing a Melody That Modulates from Major to Minor
Improvising in Compound Duple Time

1. To the melodic statement given in the Major Mode, improvise a corresponding statement in the Minor Mode. In this case, "2" is the "bridge."

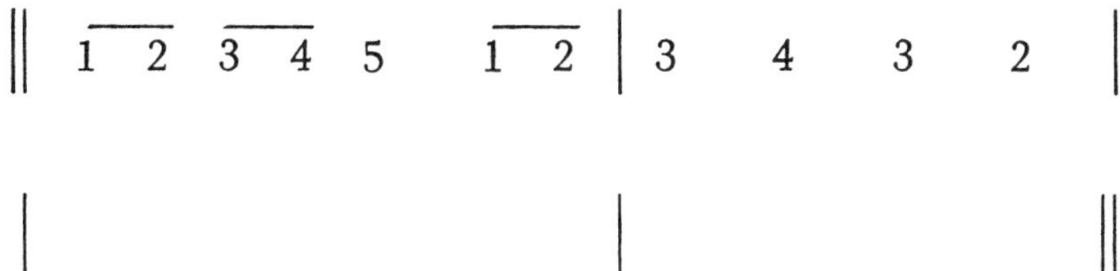


2. To the following provide an answering line in the Major Mode:

3. Improvise a melody based on the rhythms shown in Rhythm Patterns Series 15 of this lesson. DO Mode. If possible, make a transition by means of a "bridge" to the LA Mode.

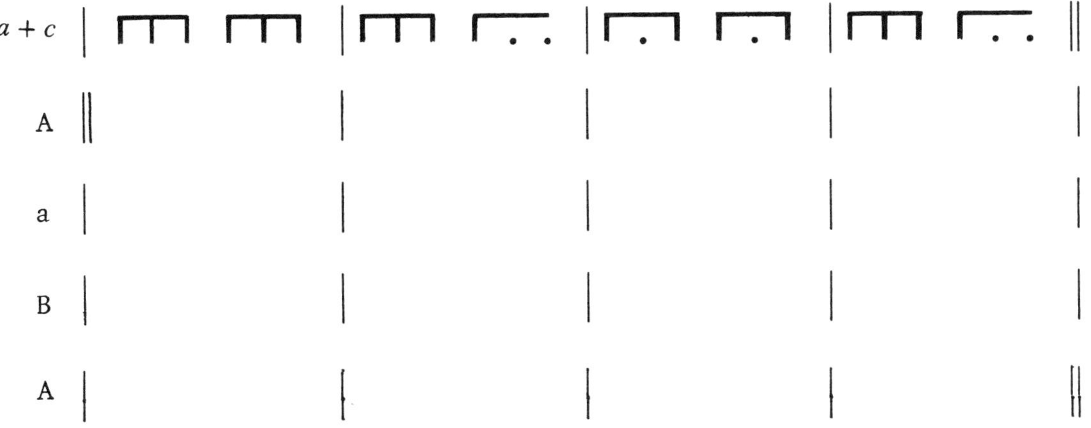


The form AaBA is only a suggestion

# Lesson 21

Bridges Between Major and Minor Modes - Continued

# Intonation

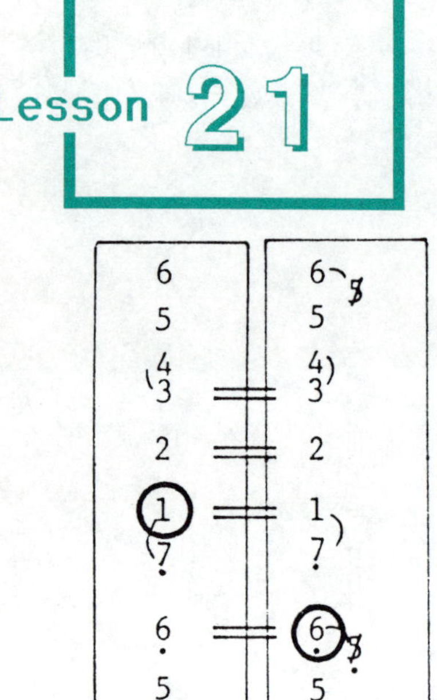


Intonation Diagram 33

Intonation Exercise 42 Crossing bridges with "think" notes as links

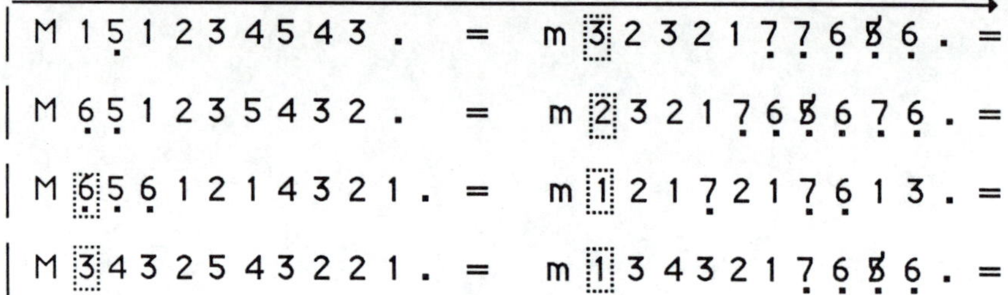


*Practice each line separately; then sing the four lines as a continuous exercise. Notice that each bridge has been crossed at least once in the exercise and that each new phrase begins on a new note after the cross-over. The "think" notes are help notes and should not be audible.*

*Use this diagram for* **THEREFORE WE BEFORE HIM BENDING** *and* **I LOVE SIXPENCE**

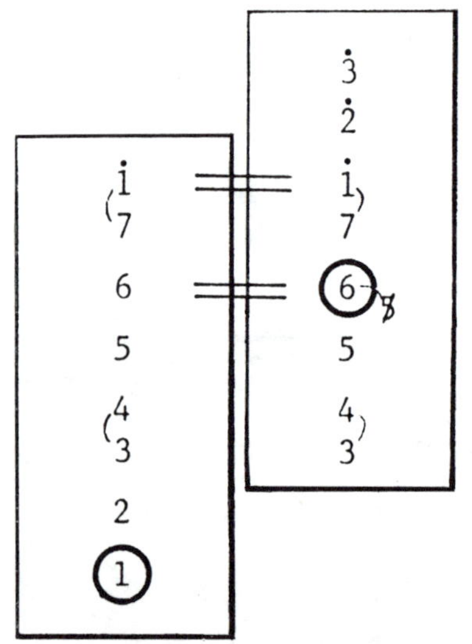


Intonation Diagram 34

Use Intonation Diagram 34 for practice of Melody No. 41 and Melody No. 43

**Dictations**

# Rhythm

Compound Duple Time Beginning on Down-Pulse 6/8
Exercise in Study of Rests in 4/4 Time

1. Rhythm Patterns **Series 16** with Metrical Gesture II and the neutral syllable "Du."

Practice each line separately several times singing the syllable "Du" to the melody given.

2. Exercise in Study of Rests in 4/4 Time

Keeping time with Metrical Gesture IV and singing each note on the neutral syllable "Du," sing the following five lines of music as one continuous exercise. Notice that in each new line rests have been substituted for notes of the preceding line. Maintain a steady tempo and make no audible sound during the rests.

## Dictations

# Notation

Exercises in Writing Rests

A melody is given in the first line below. On the second line write the equivalent time values in rests of the notes shown in the first line.

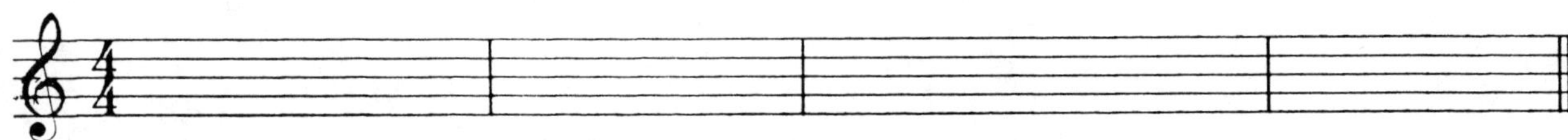

# Creative Activity

Four-Phrase Compositions with Theme "A" Given
Tonal Structure: Minor-Major-Minor
Major-Minor-Major
Form Optional

1\. M | 5 . 3 | 1 . 3 | 5 . 6 | 5 . . |
m | | | | |
m | | | | |
M | | | | ||

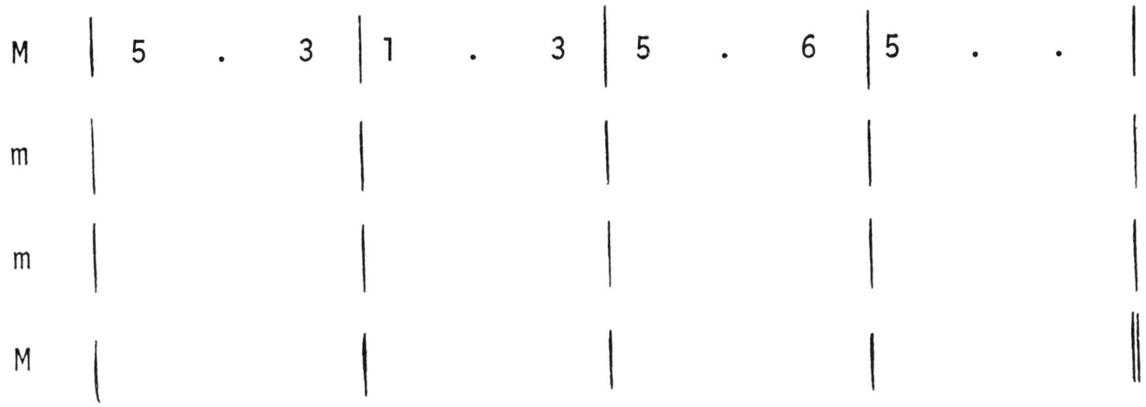

2\. m || 6 3 3 3 | 2 4 3 2 1 7 6 |
M | | |
M | | |
m | | ||

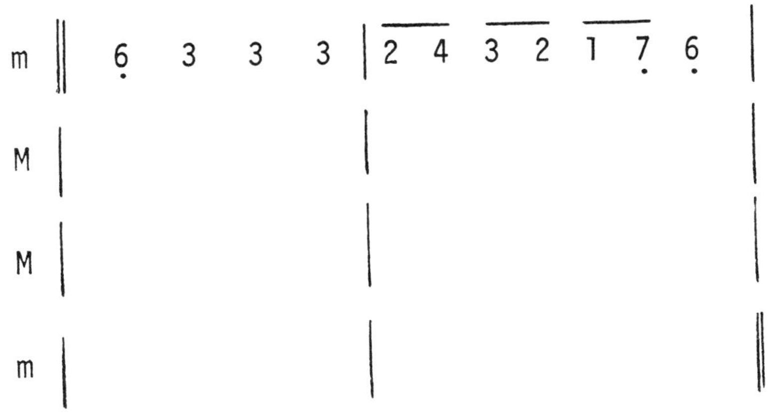

3\. Improvise a theme and a four-phrase melody in 6/8 time - DO Mode

|| | | |
| | | |
| | | |
| | | ||

Major and Minor Counterparts

# Intonation

*When a theme in one mode is reproduced in another mode, it is called a "counterpart." In the examples given below, sing each melody and then its "counterpart."*

*Each theme in the* M *(Major) column is reproduced in the* m *(minor) column by starting three notes lower.*

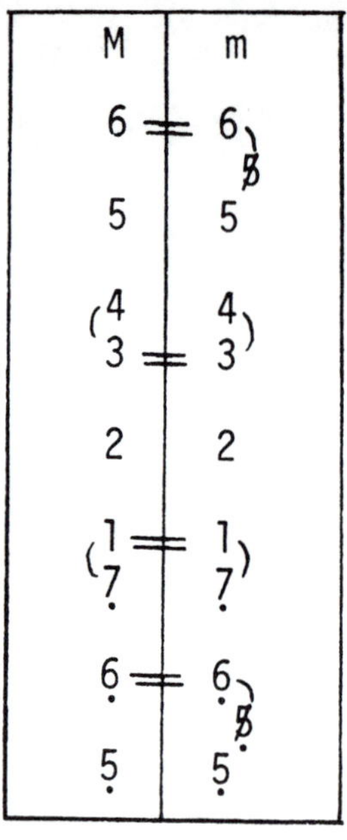


Intonation Diagram 35

‖ M 1 3 | 5 4 | 3 2 | 1 . |
| m 6 1 | 3 2 | 1 7 | 6 . ‖

‖ M 1 2 | 3 1 | 2 2 | 2 . |
| m 6 7 | 1 6 | 7 7 | 7 . ‖

‖ M 1 | 5 3 | 1 5 | 6 6 | 5 . | .
m 6 | 3 1 | 6 3 | 4 4 | 3 . | . ‖

*Each theme in the* m *(minor) column is then reproduced in the* M *(Major) column by starting three notes higher.*

‖ m 6 . 7 | 1 2 | 7 . | 6 . |
| M 1 . 2 | 3 4 | 2 . | 1 . ‖

‖ m 6 5 6 7 | 1 2 | 3 . | 6 . |
| M 1 7 1 2 | 3 4 | 5 . | 1 . ‖

**Dictations**

# Rhythm

Exercise in Study of Rests in 3/4 Time

Using Metrical Gesture III, sing the following notes on one tone with the neutral syllable "Du." Make no sound during the "rests." Sing the four lines without stopping.

# Notation

The Fermata Sign
Exercise in Writing Rests in 3/4 Time

1. *The* Fermata Sign 𝄐 *found over or beneath a note signifies a momentary cessation of the rhythmic movement. The notes that follow this sign continue to be sung in the rhythm of the song.*

*Examples:* *The last line of* **THE JOLLY MILLER**

**BREAK FORTH, O BEAUTEOUS HEAV'NLY LIGHT**

2. Transcribe the following note values to rests:

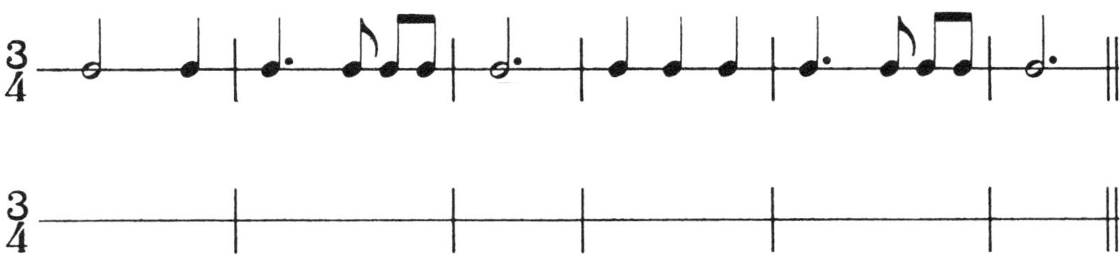

# Creative Activity

Major-Minor Counterparts

1. Lines shown below are taken from the songs of this lesson. Determine the mode of each and write its counterpart.

2. Provide a melody for the given text. Introduce a minor counterpart. Notice the syncopation in the third and fourth lines.

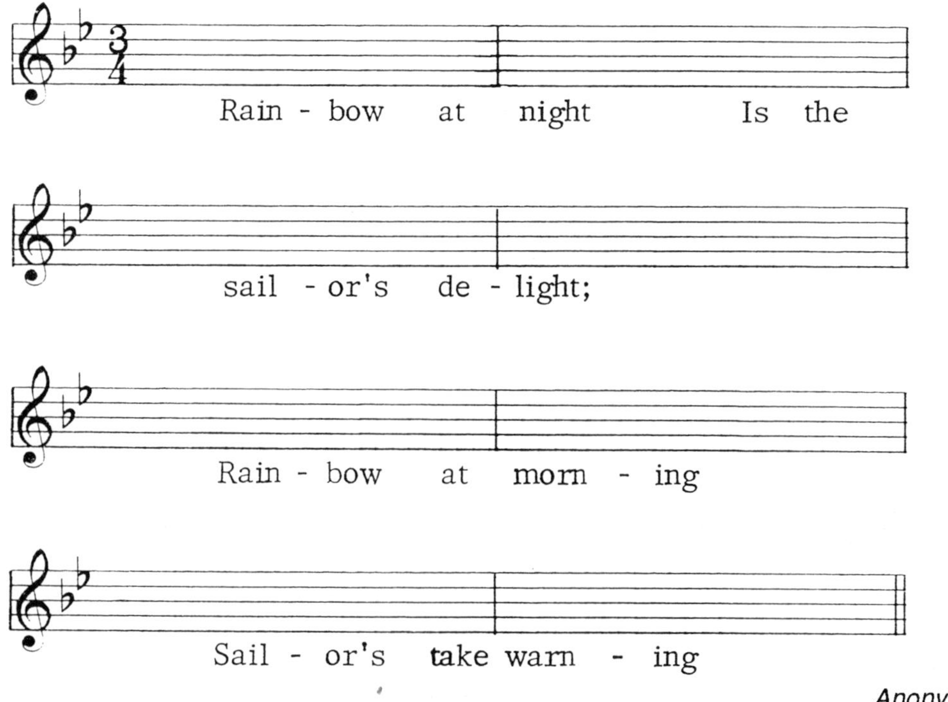


*Anonymous*

# Dictations

# Dictations

## Creative Activity

## Creative Activity